BROKEN

JUSTICE

I0116836

WHEN LAWLESS GANGS
CAPTURE THE STATE

JOE K. MUNGAI

BROKEN JUSTICE

When Lawless Gangs Capture the State

Joe K. Mungai

Copyright 2019 © Joe K. Mungai

ISBN: 978-1-7339798-0-1

Joe K. Mungai
2150 James St # 5204 Coralville
IA 52241
Ph. +1319-325-3225
Fax: +1319-338-1717
Email: contact@speakoutspeakup.life
www.speakoutspeakup.life
www.facebook.com/yourspeakout
www.twitter.com/yourspeakout

Published and distributed in the USA by:
BREMA GROUP ENTERPRISES LLC
P.O. BOX 5204 Coralville IA 52241

TABLE OF CONTENTS

DEDICATION

To the memory of my brother Edward, for the important lessons he taught me.

May his memory forever inspire us to achieve justice for all.

FOREWORD

*B*roken Justice is unique in its approach to improving social conditions and promoting social justice. It offers a compelling message, not only encouraging its readers to use available opportunities to change their life circumstances, but also teaches them how to develop those opportunities.

The insights, concepts and principles that Joe shares in this book will deepen your understanding of what it means for a community and indeed a whole society to come together and chart their own future. The message of this book will fuel your desire and inspire you to want to do more for your society. It will help you realize that there's no way you can just be a casual citizen who says nothing when society is taking a wrong turn.

Joseph was my social worker and coach for several years. He believes that when we hold ourselves back and not live our lives to our true potential, we deny future generations gifts that are invested in us, which could benefit them. If you ponder and savor the picture Joe has laid out in this book, I believe you will find it to be ravishing and powerful.

Joe enters the world of community transformation from a unique perspective, having been a social worker, a coach and a mentor. He has provided spiritual guidance to many people for many years. His counselor's heart and his ability to simplify complex issues make it easier to understand the message of this book.

Joe has had to overcome many obstacles in his own life. The loss of his brother which impacted him greatly. The message he has in his heart from that experience is evident throughout this book. His move to the United States was a huge change which involved learning a culture, and overcoming barriers in a new country. But Joseph has that special ability to learn quickly, be very open minded, and has a drive that has no equal. He is above excellent in communication, speaking and writing very clearly and precisely, and ensuring that both his listeners and readers understand his intents very well. Joseph is extremely dedicated not only to his work but also to the people he represents and looks after. He is extremely diligent and professional in every manner.

In this book, Joe takes a leadership role in nation building, facilitating dialogue in the community and society alike, and empowers his readers to take action on their own behalf.

I believe that the message in this book will challenge and equip you to become a transformational worker and a change agent in your own community.

Bruce Clark

PREFACE

My brother, Edward, was driving home from Kigango on a Sunday evening. On board his truck were three friends. He had offered them transport, to get them home, as any good friend would do. Unfortunately, as he negotiated a corner, his truck pushed one motorbike that was parked too close to the road. It was not hit, and no one was on it at the time. But it was touched by the tail side of the truck (lorry) as my brother made a turn.

Boda-boda riders came to him right away in a group and an argument erupted. My brother must have assumed that it was something they could address and resolve. If there was some damage to the motorbike, definitely the vehicle insurance would take care of that. But that was not to be, as he was dealing with a group of people who had a different mindset about how to resolve traffic issues. He was dealing with a group that has no will to solve conflicts in a civilized manner. He tried to talk to them to see how they could resolve their misunderstanding, but they were not willing to talk or to resolve it that way. They were only interested in physically attacking him. Sensing danger, he quickly drove away with an aim to get to the closest police station, which happened to be Makongeni. His would-be killers pursued him.

Edward showed heroism in a very unlikely situation. He demonstrated bravery and selflessness to ensure the safety of his friends. One of his friends requested him to slow down, for him to alight. Remember Edward was fleeing from a murderous gang that was chasing his truck. But he was magnanimous enough, he slowed down, and the friend alighted. Most likely, the friend sensed that the marauding gang would not stop at anything to carry out their evil scheme, therefore he wanted to get away as fast as possible, which he did. Edward drove on after his friend alighted, but more trouble lay ahead. Just before getting to Garissa Road, which he needed to join and then make a right turn in order to get to the police station, which was just few feet away, he saw a second group of *boda-boda* riders coming towards him. They were on their bikes, with full lights on (it was late evening). We learnt later that this second group had been contacted by the first group, which Edward had left behind, with instructions to block the road to prevent Edward from reaching the police station. The riders knew my brother, and could recognize his truck. This second group transports passengers from Makongeni to Kiganjo. The first group transports passengers from Kiganjo to Makongeni.

My brother must have been fully aware of the imminent danger facing him and his two remaining passengers. There was no doubt that the gang's aim was to physically attack him, which for the murderous gang is nothing more than a casual undertaking. My brother attempted to make a quick turn on his right to get to a back road which he could use to get to the police station. Unfortunately, the road was narrow, and because my brother had been speeding, so as to get away from the gang that was pursuing him as quickly as possible, as he made the turn, the truck hit an electric post at the corner of the junction. That had the effect of immobilizing the truck. The *boda-boda* gang, like a pack of wolves that has caught the scent of blood, descended on him and overwhelmed him.

Edward died a gruesome death.

Why did he die? Because his truck knocked on an unmanned motorbike that had been parked too close to the road.

INTRODUCTION

"Leadership is not a position. Leadership is not a title. Leadership is influence. You are a leader if you act responsibly no matter where or what the issue is." - Joe K. Mungai

I have written this book to expose the actions of the self-styled gang that comprises *boda-boda* riders, and the evil collusion that exists between this gang and law enforcement agencies, to frustrate justice in Kenya.

My brother was killed by members of this gang way back in November, 2015. There is no way anyone can reasonably explain failure by the government to prosecute at least one person, to date, for that heinous crime. The only reason why the murderers have not faced justice in a court of law is because these criminals are partners-in-crime with law enforcement agencies. That is one of the consequences that befall communities that are riddled with corruption.

Perhaps you have come across an analogy that has been cited to demonstrate the gulf between the attitude of a leader of a developed state, and the attitude of leaders of failed states and others that have stagnated, a good number of which are in the African continent.

It is said that when the Prime Minister of Singapore, Lee Kuan Yew, assumed leadership of his country, he realized that he had two options. The same is true of our African leaders when we elect them into office. The options are, one, become corrupt; or two, serve the country.

The response below is attributed to Lee Kuan Yew. Compare the choice he made to the choice many African leaders make when presented with the same scenario.

There were two options for me, said the Prime Minister of Singapore: either I get corrupted and put my family in the Forbes list of the richest people in the world and leave my country with nothing;
OR

Serve my country and my people and help my country be in the list of the best ten economies in the world.

I chose the second option.

African politicians said, "There were two options for us too, but the second option was already taken by the Prime Minister of Singapore."

The words might come out as a joke, but they have a lot of truth in them. Painful as it is, we must admit that many of our leaders have chosen the first option. They are busy not building their countries but amassing a fortune for themselves.

Unfortunately, and regrettably, many Kenyans have joined the cabal of corrupt leaders, instead of remaining true to that which they know is best for the country.

I know that it is frustrating to try to fix anything in Kenya. I know it, because I have experienced it many times. But one thing I haven't done and I will not do, is to give up on my homeland. I still believe in its potential and the goodwill of its people. We shouldn't give up doing what we know to be the right thing to do. Each of us must use our influence for the good of our country. Your belief in the potential of our country will keep you going. It will keep you committed to doing that which promotes the welfare of our country and its citizens.

Why is it frustrating to fix anything in Kenya?

Here is the reason. I will use a metaphor I came across sometimes back to explain the frustration.

> *I know that it is frustrating to try to fix anything in Kenya. I know it, because I have experienced it many times. But one thing I haven't done and I will not do, is to give up on my homeland. I still believe in its potential and the goodwill of its people. We shouldn't give up doing what we know to be the right thing to do. Each of us must use our influence for the good of our country. Your belief in the potential of our country will keep you going.*

Kenya is like a vehicle. While you are fixing the brain box, someone has removed the tires. When you are done fixing the tires, you discover that the brake system has been damaged and you have to do something about it. When you are done fixing it, you find out that the battery has been stolen.

When you are done with those and have replaced the stolen battery and you are about to start the engine, you realize that the kick-starter is faulty. You fix the kick-starter, but then you discover that the plugs are gone.

When you are done with all these fixes, and you are finally about to move – it's taken a whole day, so it's already dusk – you realize that the headlight bulbs are dead too. While trying to figure that out, it begins to rain. Unfortunately, the wipers are old so you cannot wipe the rain water that is cascading on the windscreen. For your own safety, you decide to park the car and sit out until the ebbing of the downpour. You attempt to roll up the windows, but unfortunately the power controls aren't working.

This is the madness that we see every day in our country. A group will be stealing some things as one is fixing a section of the vehicle.

That's the frustration one can sometimes face while trying to fix anything in Kenya. The leadership is bad and the followership is super-bad! Why do I say that the followership is super-bad? Strange thinking patterns have taken root, giving rise to miserable mindsets. The same people whose lives have been sabotaged by a small clique of corrupt individuals join them to become saboteurs and fellow accomplices.

As we look at the challenges facing our country, I encourage you to respond by making a commitment to be part of the group that will enforce the change our country urgently needs. Do not sit on the fence, but instead come on board. As a good soldier who is ready for battle, stand up to be counted and let's fix our country together.

PART 1

FRAMING
THE PROBLEM

In this section, I will start by showing you what is happening in our country when it comes to dealing with our law courts and the law enforcement system at large. I will use myself and my family as an example and show you what a lot of Kenyans are experiencing in terms of not being accorded justice that is due to them. This will give you a taste of our broken justice system that is frustrating millions of Kenyans every day in various ways, and eventually denying them justice that they so desperately deserve.

A broken justice system allows the government to oppress its people in very many ways using the same systems that are supposed to help them. What I share here is just one of the ways our government is using to frustrate our quest for justice. It's a very painful ordeal, which I am sure many families have experienced at one time or another, with some of them experiencing it right now even as you read these words.

As a family, we would not have expected our very own government to frustrate our quest for justice, given the fact that the case is about the cold-blooded murder of our brother by a group of *boda-boda* riders. No grieving family should suffer the kind of frustrations we have had to bear.

In this section, I will also share insights about what can be referred to as the philosophy of the *boda-boda* riders, who have evolved into a home-grown gang of criminals. Unfortunately and very regrettably, our government has handed its authority to this home-grown terrorist group, allowing it to terrorize the population, with impunity.

Additionally, I also share the nature of my brother's death, a heinous crime that was methodically carried out by members of a *boda-boda* group in Kiganjo-Makongeni, in Thika.

Finally, I'll share the lessons that my brother's death has taught me about the incompetence of our police force. That incompetence isn't just confined to the police force; it spreads through the entire justice system.

CHAPTER 1

JUSTICE DENIED

Corn can't expect justice from a court composed of chickens.
– African Proverb

The big question that still lingers in my mind after the despicable crime that took my brother's life is, why haven't the authorities arrested the killers? Why are they still roaming free? Are the authorities waiting for those criminals to take out another innocent life, and another, and another? How many deaths, such as the one suffered by my brother, will it take to spur the authorities to action?

I just want to make sure that other people's lives are spared. I know that punishing those who murdered my brother will not bring him back to life, but if justice is seen to be done, people's faith in the legal system will be restored.

How has my family been denied justice?

Three years after the murder of my brother, I still wait for justice. I feel like my brother's murderers are being rewarded by the government of Kenya through Thika Police Station and a court system that is delaying and denying us justice that we are entitled to. No steps have been taken to bring the perpetrators to book. Even worse than justice that has been delayed is the knowledge that his murderers have not been arrested. They have been left to roam free and kill again. Those who were initially arrested were let go by the police without the knowledge of the court.

Spare No Details

Some of the people who killed my brother were apprehended by members of the community. My family shielded them from being killed by members of the public. During the time when those individuals were under the custody of community members, my family talked to them and asked them to spare no details in describing the circumstances in which my brother died. Their account was collaborated by an eye witness who let everyone know how my brother was killed.

It's incredible how much information we have about how my brother died, yet it has not been used by the relevant government agencies to bring those who killed him to justice. The police have most of the details since the criminals who killed my brother were handed over to them. They gave information which detailed how the murderous attack was carried out. My family and those close to the family have that information. Those who were apprehended by members of the public revealed the names of the other *boda-boda* riders who participated in killing my brother.

The three police stations, that is, Thika (where the case was reported); Makongeni (where my brother was yanked from his truck and thereafter killed by the *boda-boda* riders); and Kiganjo, (where my brother was driving from), are all informed, but they have refused to act.

I can see the effect of the bungled justice process on my parents and the entire family. But they have refused to buckle. I find that really admirable. They are hurting, but they know they have to cope.

Make no mistake about it; members of my family are plagued by questions. I know they are haunted by thoughts of why it happened the way it happened. But it's even more hurting and traumatizing when you think what the government has done – denying us justice.

I have experienced loss before, but Edward's death was particularly tragic and brutal. His life was quickly taken away from him so violently. He would be living a fulfilling and worthwhile life right now.

Edward's brutal murder was carried out by *boda-boda* riders who ferry members of the public between Kiganjo and Makongeni. The murder happened at Makongeni Phase 5 on Sunday, 22nd November 2015.

The head of criminal investigations is aware of the case but has not done anything tangible.

My family contacted the Independent Police Oversight

Authority (IPOA) on June 9th, 2016, when nothing seemed coming from the police.

IPOA contacted the Directorate of Criminal Investigations (DCI) on August 5th, 2016. The DCI was asked by IPOA to respond to the family, giving them an update of the case, detailing the steps that have been taken. The DCI responded within a few days in the same month of August and reported that the court was taking action, and that a court date had been scheduled for August 16th, 2016.

What should have already happened nine months earlier became possible in less than a month. That happened because questions were posed to the DCI about the murder. Note, that the DCI responded because someone else (IPOA), in addition to the family, posed questions about the murder. The DCI authorized action to be taken by the court right away. If the family never wrote to IPOA, and if IPOA never wrote to the DCI, no steps would have been taken by Kenya's justice system to address the brutal murder of my brother by a criminal gang.

Can you imagine living your life in a place like this, or raising your children here?

What is the difference between the killers and those who are supposed to stop them from killing (law enforcement agencies), if they are doing nothing to bring the killers to justice?

I can see the effect of the bungled justice process on my parents and the entire family. But they have refused to buckle. I find that really admirable. They are hurting, but they know they have to cope. Make no mistake about it; members of my family are plagued by questions. I know they are haunted by thoughts of why it happened the way it happened. But it's even more hurting and traumatizing when you think what the government has done – denying us justice.

This is how you empower a gang. This is how a government hands over power to a gang of criminals and allows it to decide who should die, and who should live. This is what our government has done. How else would you explain the unwillingness by government agencies to act? These are the people we have entrusted to take care of us. These are the government agencies that are entrusted with the future of our children, and that of our children's children. Prior to this communication, my family had never received any updates on the investigations, or when a hearing was scheduled to happen. But all of a sudden, after IPOA wrote to the DCI, we were informed that action by the court was now underway.

Is this how Kenya's criminal investigation system works?

What a shame!

But wait; we are not out of the woods yet. Even with a court date, we still have a problem, a huge problem that the DCI is not aware of. A problem created by the police officers. I will tell you about this in a minute, but what I tell you next will shock you.

We are going to have a judge and a prosecutor in a court room, but without a single defendant. No one has been accused or charged with the murder of my brother. The question you are bound to ask is, what happened to my brother's killers? Members of the community apprehended some of them and handed them over to the police, others were arrested by the police a week after my brother was murdered. How come none of them would be in the court room?

Up to the time of the court appearance that the DCI ordered to happen, the police had not charged anyone with my brother's murder. This means there was no one to appear in the court room as a suspect.

Can you put yourself in my family's shoes and imagine what was going through our minds when we realized that a scheduled court date was going to take place without anyone being arraigned as a suspect, leave alone being charged with the heinous murder of my brother?

It is hard to put what we felt in words. As a family, we were encouraged when we learned that a court date had been fixed. We expected this was going to kick-start the process of serving justice. I assumed that the various arms of the criminal justice system were working together, to get the case moving. I was shocked to learn that the DCI had no background understanding of the case. All he knew was what he had heard from the family through IPOA. Apparently, he wasn't aware of collusion by staff in his unit to sabotage the case. I was more than disappointed. I was furious, seeing the level of incompetence and the extent of corruption in our criminal justice system.

How could a director fix a date for a court date without first making sure that everything is in order?

There is a term you might not be familiar with, because it's not a term you hear often. The term is, *inquest*.

An inquest, according to a dictionary definition, *is when a court of law or a coroner investigates the circumstances of a person's death.* An inquest is typically carried out when there is something unexplained or suspicious about the circumstances in which someone died. This mostly happens in case a death is deemed to have happened unnaturally or accidentally. What this implies, is that the occurrence of death doesn't always call for an inquest.

So, instead of holding a hearing, what the court ended up doing was hold an inquest. But a very different kind of inquest. The kind of inquest that happened at Thika, in my opinion, was a *cover up inquest*. Why do I call it a cover up inquest?

This is why; why would a court of law use its time to try to figure out how my brother died when there was an eye-witness account of how he died and who killed him? Why would an inquest be held to try to find out what the police already knew? They had all the details about the grim murder of my brother, but those details were not presented at the inquest. The doctor who conducted the autopsy wrote a report detailing how my brother died and what caused his death. I have a copy of the report. Details of that report were not submitted at the inquest. If you don't involve those who know what you want to know, it can only be that the process you are engaged in is a cover up.

One of the arresting police officer in this case was present when the autopsy was conducted. His name is in the report of the copy in my possession. The name of the doctor who conducted the autopsy is also in the report. I didn't have to point that out, because it's obvious. But apparently, it wasn't obvious to the officer who ordered that a court date be convened without first making sure that everything needed was in place. It wasn't obvious also to the judge and the prosecutor who held an inquest without first making sure they had the right people in the room.

Is this how Kenyan courts work?

This is so sad for all of us, because it shows how as a society we have embraced corruption. It also shows how the agencies that are tasked to serve justice have lost sight of their role.

Autopsy

The doctor who conducted the autopsy stated that:

1. The deceased had been beaten with all manner of crude weapons, occasioning his death.
2. He also noted, among others:
3. Fractured skull with several cuts from blunt and sharp weapons.
4. Multiple cut wounds and abrasion on the face and scalp.
5. Several broken bones.
6. Several fractured teeth.
7. Multiple cuts on the lips.
8. Multiple cuts on the fingers causing amputation.

Such was the cruelty that my brother was subjected to. We were informed that one of the *boda-boda* riders who resides near the place where my brother was killed was called by his fellow gang members, and he came out with a *rungu* (club), which he used to clobber my brother, breaking his ribs and teeth, and fracturing one side of his head. That verbal report is well collaborated by the findings of the doctor who conducted the autopsy.

What kind of people would do this to another human being? My brother was not a robber or a criminal. He was not an animal to die a cold-blooded death like this.

If the government has surrendered its power and given it to this homegrown criminal gang, allowing it to terrorize and kill Kenyans in this manner, it may as well give them guns, which might be less torturous than the crude weapons used by barbaric gangs in their dark and twisted world.

The question that has remained unanswered is, why was no one charged? Why has no one been charged? I will answer the question. As a matter of fact, the only reason the case never took off and remains in limbo, to date, is because the police let the criminals go free after receiving a bribe. You heard right; the police received a bribe and let the murderers off the hook. That is why we are in the mess that we are in. That is why the DCI, the judge and the prosecutor are embarrassed. But they won't accept it, they won't come out and say, *we know where the problem is.*

When the police made the arrest and gathered the details of how my brother was killed, there is something they intentionally didn't do; they never charged anyone with the crime that led to the death of my brother. The prosecutor wasn't given the file as needed to prosecute the case. There was no report or record of the findings of the police in regard to the case. Police officers who investigated the crime took a bribe and let the murderers go free.

This is why there was a court date that had a judge and a prosecutor present, but no report from the officers who investigated the case. According to the police, the file got lost.

After that inquest – the cover up inquest that produced nothing – the case went cold and fell off the cliff. There were no further investigations or rearrests, or arrests. There was no report or assistance from the police anymore. Everybody was thrown off.

I flew to Kenya from the US and met the Assistant to Head of Criminal Investigations at Thika Police Station face to face in January, 2017. I asked for an update regarding the case. He told me, "We cannot find the file of your brother's murder."

That is not what you want to hear from a senior law enforcement officer in regard to a matter that touches the very core of your life. I was in that office to find out what the police were doing to bring the criminals who had killed my brother to justice. Surely, the Assistant to Head of Criminal Investigations knew better.

My body temperature started to rise, and my blood began to boil. I thought I would explode, but another thought told me to calm down. But seriously, how do you lose a file? A whole file? Just like that?

I had hoped for positive feedback, detailing the work that the police had undertaken to fix what they had messed up, only to be more disappointed.

There are two things that I want to see happen; one, I am seeking for a closure. I want to see my brother's killers in court. I want to be able to give a victim statement at the court of law with everyone present, including my brother's killers. I want to tell them how they have devastated our family. We can't have closure without having the truth come out in the open.

There are two things that I want to see happen; one, I am seeking for a closure. I want to see my brother's killers in court. I want to be able to give a victim statement at the court of law with everyone present, including my brother's killers. I want to tell them how they have devastated our family. We can't have closure without having the truth come out in the open.

In a situation like this, a court can only start an inquest, but this time, the inquest should be about **what went wrong.** Why do I say that? Because all other questions have been answered. Questions about how my brother died or who killed him have been answered. All that is left for the court to figure out is, *what went wrong?* Why did the police not charge those criminals right away? How is it that the court has no paper work detailing aspects of the murder that everyone knows about? Then, the court should ponder what its role is. How can it restore people's faith in the legal system in Kenya? A nation whose justice system is corrupt becomes a nation of criminals who violate with abandon all laws known to man.

An upright judicial and law enforcement system provides a net that catches violators and brings them to justice. It also provides speedy trials and severe punishment to those caught for crime they have committed, or crime that they are conspiring to commit. That sends a message to those who would be violators of law.

No member of the judicial and law enforcement system should allow criminals to harass the public. And no member of the justice system should prevent a guilty verdict from being entered against criminals. There has to be widespread and general determination to sweep out of the way those things that foster the spirit of bribery so as to defeat the cause of justice, and denial of justice to those who deserve it.

CHAPTER 2

THE CULTURE AND PHILOSOPHY OF *BODA-BODA*

"There is no law for boda-boda organizing, save the Law of the Jungle."
– Joe K. Mungai

What is the guiding philosophy of this home-grown gang of criminals?

One thing is clear about this group when it comes to its operations; they operate on jungle laws, or the Law of the Wolves.

I will use a poem here below to paint the picture of what I mean by Law of the Wolves. Wolves and *boda-boda* riders share many similarities, because who they are becomes clear when they are in a group. That is when they are most violent and brutal, and casually break every law known to man. They still carry the seeds of lawlessness even when they operate individually, but it's when they are together that their true selves emerge.

Rudyard Kipling, poet, used the phrase *Law of the Jungle* to describe the obligations and behavior of a wolf when in a pack. There is so much to learn from this description if you are interested in understanding how *boda-boda* riders behave, and why they feel obligated towards each other.

The Law of the Wolves
Now this is the law of the jungle, as old and as true as the sky,
And the wolf that shall keep it may prosper, but the wolf that shall break it must die.

As the creeper that girdles the tree trunk, the law runneth forward and back;

For the strength of the pack is the wolf, and the strength of the wolf is the pack.
Wash daily from nose tip to tail tip; drink deeply, but never too deep;
And remember the night is for hunting and forget not the day is for sleep.

The jackal may follow the tiger, but, cub, when thy whiskers are grown,
Remember the wolf is a hunter – go forth and get food of thy own.

Keep peace with the lords of the jungle, the tiger, the panther, the bear;
And trouble not Hath the Silent, and mock not the boar in his lair.

When pack meets with pack in the jungle, and neither will go from the trail,
Lie down till the leaders have spoken; it may be fair words shall prevail.

When ye fight with a wolf of the pack ye must fight him alone and afar,
Lest others take part in the quarrel and the pack is diminished by war.
– **Rudyard Kipling (1865–1936)**

Gang Philosophy

What is the philosophy of this home-grown gang of criminals?

I'll start by letting you know that the *boda-boda* business group is not just about making an income; many members are in it for very varied purposes – to destroy, steal, hurt, maim and kill Kenyans. They are also in the *boda-boda* enterprise for politicians to hire them to do their dirty work. Being in this business allows them to be in one pool where they can be accessed and tapped by our leaders for dirty work.

Many of *Boda-boda* riders are beyond any human decency that you know of.

Their inability to behave and live like human beings is incomprehensible.

Their inability to empathize or see things from anyone else's perspective other than their own is sickening. These people are not fit to be on the streets. As a matter of fact, the government is putting your life in danger by allowing them to be out in the public.

What they need is rehabilitation, which for them is in the criminal justice system, not in the community where the rest of the society is.

A Sampling of their Philosophy

There have been gangs that successive governments have allowed to flourish in the past. Whatever guides them in doing what they do as a group is what I call their philosophy.

Let me give an overview of the culture of this gang before I unpack its philosophy.

Members of this gang are mostly related by friendship. They would like members of the public to believe that they derive their income from the *boda-boda* business. However, as earlier indicated, there are other non-economic motives for the existence of the *boda-boda* gangs. This is what makes them dangerous.

As a gang, members of this group spend considerable time hanging out together not only when they are offering transport services to the community, but also after they are done working. Their time together involves verbal sparring and a myriad of social activities. This is where the cohesiveness of the group is formed. Crime is less than a full-time activity for them. Moreover, instead of resorting to violence if they have to – for rational reasons, like defending themselves if they are wronged – most of their violence against other road users and members of the public happens merely for fun or to make a name among themselves.

The *boda-boda* gang isn't just another bunch of law-breakers. This is a fierce and barbarous gang that butchers people without giving their actions a second thought. You should not forget that any time you encounter them.

They believe that they control the streets and the roads. They believe that Kenya has no traffic laws – except the laws that these gang members choose to implement. Sadly, they have pocketed the police force. And since they work for our leaders to get them into the offices they hold, through campaigning for them, they (boda-boda gangs) behave as if they own constitutional power in the country. Our leaders might think they own the power, but they don't. What the leaders don't understand is that the moment they incorporated the boda-boda gangs in their campaigns, they gave these gang members leverage to exercise their brutal power. They, not elected officials, own power. That is how the boda-boda gangs blackmail our leaders.

They also believe that they are above the law. Police keep filing reports of complaints by the public, and promise to take action against them, but nothing happens. Maybe the gang members are right after all; the country is governed by jungle laws, defined by The Oxford English Dictionary as "the code of survival in jungle life, with reference to the superiority of brute force or self-interest in the struggle for survival."

This criminal gang believes that the constitution of Kenya and the laws of the land do not protect members

This criminal gang believes that the constitution of Kenya and the laws of the land do not protect members of the public from the violence that the gang unleashes on them. They believe that they can maim and kill a member of the public with whom they disagree and not face any consequences. They are of the view that it's acceptable to use violence to prevent a member of the public from accessing law enforcement agencies to report lawlessness or seek safety.

of the public from the violence that the gang unleashes on them. They believe that they can maim and kill a member of the public with whom they disagree and not face any consequences. They are of the view that it's acceptable to use violence to prevent a member of the public from accessing law enforcement agencies to report lawlessness or seek safety.

Why is this so?

It's because they believe they have the power over everyone else in Kenya. Already, they have succeeded in striking fear in the hearts of Kenyans. I will give you three examples to prove this point. Much of this is what you see daily on Kenyan streets.

1. **Members of the public are unable to defend each other.** It's not unusual these days to see *boda-boda* riders attacking their own passengers, or a member of the public, or a motor vehicle driver, with members of the public helplessly looking on. As I shared before, this is because *boda-boda* riders have become a potent force of evil that is destroying traditional Kenyan values that move us to help each other.

    The public is therefore powerless and at the mercy of *boda-boda* riders who, like wolves, come together to eliminate what they see as a challenge to them. The threat posed by this gang is fuelled by the unwillingness of the law enforcement agencies to defend and uphold the rights of all Kenyans.

2. **Well-meaning people are afraid to call for help when a fellow member of the society is being attacked by *boda-boda* riders.** My brother Edward Ng'ang'a Mungai had three companions with him when he was pursued and attacked. But none of them dared to help him or seek help for him. They didn't report what had happened, in spite of the fact that there was a police station just a few feet away. They just walked away from the scene. They could have walked to the police station to report the crime they had witnessed. But they chose not to.

    This is what I mean when I say that *boda-boda* riders have struck fear into the hearts of Kenyans.

    How do you walk away from a man who is pleading for your help to get him out of the hands of an evil gang? How do you choose to do nothing and just walk away? The man has done everything he could to get you home safely at night. Now he needs you. A murderous gang is ripping him apart. Would you not help him?

The three loved their lives more than Edward's, so they were just happy to be spared (the boda-boda gang let them go saying, we want the driver). They loved their lives more than Edward's, so they just walked away and did nothing after that.

You can imagine what I felt when I learned this from those accompanying my brother before he was killed. He was helping these individuals (he was driving them home when the tragedy occurred). My brother offered to get them home. One of the individuals worked in Kiganjo but lived in Makongeni. The second one was a freelance mechanic who was returning back home from Kiganjo. He also lived in Makongeni. The third person had accompanied Edward to escort the other two and then return home together. Edward was helping these people get home after working late in the evening.

They did not just fail to help him. Worse than that, they never went to seek help for him. They never alerted the police about what was happening a few feet's away from the police station. They never called or contacted

> *The unwillingness of our leaders to enforce the law makes the public believe that the leaders' philosophy is in tandem with that of the gangs. I know that our leaders wouldn't want to hear this, but why are we talking about these things now? How did we get here? If our law enforcement agencies and elected leaders don't hold the same views the murderous gangs hold, why do they allow the gangs to flout the rule of law with impunity? Why do they allow the despicable acts of violence to continue happening on their watch?*

anyone, not even our family.

3. **Police collusion with *boda-boda* gangs is discouraging the public from reporting criminal actions.** Majority of people are afraid that if they report the criminal actions of the *boda-boda* riders to the police, the police might pass on their identity to the criminals, which would in effect put their lives in grave danger. Most members of public are aware that a section of police collude with *boda-boda* gangs. This makes members of the public shy away and keep mum, even when they are aware of the atrocities committed by the gangs.

If you go to Kiganjo Village, for example, it's easy to get a long list of unreported incidents of crime committed by the *boda-boda* riders. The silence by members of the public has emboldened the gangs to act with impunity. They (gangs) know that their evil actions won't be reported, and because they have police protection, they continue unleashing terror on the helpless public.

But you know, if the government would rise to the occasion, this would change. The government can reverse the current trend that has members of the public living in fear of the gangs; the government has everything it needs to protect the public. If police officers stop colluding with *boda-boda* gangs, members of the public will trust the police, and report criminal activities to them.

Boda-boda riders are unfriendly to other road users. The fact that majority of them are employed, meaning they don't own the motorbikes, causes them to imagine that they're despised by other road users. They think that the reason they don't have is because others have or have taken away everything (including their share), therefore they feel cheated and used.

Sadly, the employers of the *boda-boda* riders share in the same culture and philosophy with their employees – the *boda-boda* gangs. They, like their employees, treat the constitution and rule of law with contempt. How else do you explain the fact that the owners of the motorbikes don't lay-off the riders when they hurt or kill pedestrians, or passengers? What do the business owners do? They bribe the police and make them look the other way. The employers give no regard to human life as long as their employees bring them a profit.

The unwillingness of our leaders to enforce the law makes the public believe that the leaders' philosophy is in tandem with that of the gangs. I know that our leaders wouldn't want to hear this, but why are we talking about these things now? How did we get here? If our law enforcement agencies and elected leaders don't hold the same views the murderous gangs hold, why do they allow the gangs to flout the rule of law with impunity? Why do they allow the despicable acts of violence to continue happening on their watch?

The community is willing to cooperate with the police, which is essential, but what is happening in reality is that the community is cooperating with the criminals. How does this happen? They cooperate with criminals by failing to report to the authorities if and when their rights get violated. Why is this the case? As I have explained earlier, our legal authorities are perceived to be acting in cahoots with the criminals, who are capable of nasty reprisals. It is important to bear in mind that the major deterrent to crime is not an active police presence, but rather the presence of knowledgeable civilians who are prepared to report criminal activities and cooperate with the police. The criminals know that, which explains the fear they have instilled in the public, so as to keep members of the public from relaying information, which would incriminate the criminals, to the police. To a large extent, the criminals have succeeded in alienating the public from the police. Once again, as indicated earlier, the schemes of these criminals flourish because they (criminals) have found a partner in the police. This collusion is as clear as daylight.

Why doesn't the government act to cut off the evil cord? Is the whole government structure a partner in crime? The biggest losers in this convoluted scheme are members of the public, who are made to bear emotional pain that can irreversibly damage their mental as well as physical health, in addition to all the money they waste in pursuing cases that the state is not willing to resolve.

CHAPTER 3

THE NATURE OF MY BROTHER'S DEATH

"Time and circumstances can change any time. Don't devalue or hurt anyone in life. You might be powerful today. But remember, time is more powerful than you. So be good and do good."
– Joe K. Mungai

They killed my brother worse than one would kill an animal.

In some countries, like the United States, even animals have rights that protect them from cruel and unjust suffering during the process of killing them.

The manner in which my brother died was no less extreme than his unwarranted death.

You might find some of the details in this chapter disturbing. I shared some of the information in this chapter earlier, in the preface. I tell it all as those who saw it happen, reported. The violence that was unleashed on my brother was inhuman and brutal.

In November 2018, we marked the 3rd anniversary of the death of my brother, Edward Nganga Mungai. He was murdered by Kiganjo *boda-boda* riders at Makongeni, in Thika, on November 22, 2015.

The people of Kiganjo, in Thika, where my home is, caught some of my brother's killers a day or two after the heinous murder. They were going to lynch them, but my family restrained the public from killing them, opting instead to hand them over to the police. My family hoped that those who had been apprehended by members of the public would provide information that would lead to the arrest of their accomplices who were still at large. Our intention was to get all of them arraigned before a court of law. We wanted to stop the senseless maiming and killing of people in our community. There are many who had been attacked and maimed by the same group of *boda-boda* riders. Maybe their only luck, and the reason why they did not die like my brother, was because they were attacked during the day, which might have placed a restraint on the attackers, unlike my brother who was attacked at night. I had personally talked to the victims and their families and listened to them even before my brother's death. I shared their concerns with the leadership of this region. But nothing much came out of it. Some local leaders, including the officer commanding Thika Police Station seemed incensed by the awareness I was raising in the community through a local newspaper.

> *Boda-boda gangs do exactly what terrorists do. What do terrorists do? They enter a building, kill people, then change into another set of clothes and raise their hands up, pretending to be victims caught up in the attack. Security personnel sometimes end up helping the terrorists escape from the same mess they have created. That is exactly the same thing that boda-boda gangs do. They create a false impression in order to get sympathy from the public. They make the public think that they (gang) have been wronged.*

My family also reasoned that, lynching those who had been arrested would not solve the tragedy that had already taken place. This is the same way they killed my brother. Why use the same style that we know is wrong, when there's the judicial laid-down path of seeking justice? Two wrongs don't make a right. Interestingly, my brother met his death when he was attempting to use the laid-down path of solving a simple traffic misunderstanding. He was driving to the police station in search of a legal way to solve a misunderstanding between him and the *boda-boda* riders. He tried to talk to them to try resolve their misunderstanding, but they were not willing to find an amicable solution. They were only interested in physically attacking him. He then chose to remove himself from the area and quickly drove his truck away, with an intention to get to the nearest police station. But his would-be killers pursued and acting in collaboration with another boda-boda gang not far away, they blocked his way and prevented him from getting there.

I pointed out earlier, that members of public arrested some of the men who killed my brother. Before the men were handed over to the police, they narrated how they killed my brother. That's how we got the information I am going to share with you, here. This is the same information the police also got as they interviewed the killers. But the police have not shown any interest to prosecute the case. Why? The police at Thika Police station were bribed to let the killers go free before the case ever got to court.

The same police who were supposed to file charges against these killers let them go scot free. The same police that my family opted to hand over the criminals to, with the intention of protecting more people in the community from harm. Those same police do not see it that way. They don't think justice deserves to be pursued. Or that, keeping the public safe is something they should concern themselves with. These are the same police that proudly call themselves UTUMISHI KWA WOTE (SERVICE TO ALL). But instead of doing what their motto signifies, they impede the cause of justice and serve only those who line their pockets and wallets with bribes.

It is important that you know, that you are on your own. Your government does not seem to care about you, your family or your neighbor. None of the levels of government cares about your safety. If the gangs knew that the government cares about your safety, they wouldn't unleash the terror they unleash on the public, with abandon.

Let me now tell you how my brother got killed. This is what we were told.

Edward was holding on to the steering wheel of his vehicle as tight as he could, as they pulled him out of the vehicle. He was hoping, with every passing second, that help would come. Realizing that he was physically stronger than they thought, they used a machete (*panga*) to slash his fingers in order to get him to let go of the steering wheel. Next, they violently uprooted him from his seat and let him fall unaided, from the truck driver's cabin, to the ground. Then they dragged him away from his truck to the place they were going to kill him. They moved him away from his truck so as to conceal their actions from the people passing by. That is a tactic that these murderous gangs use. When they attack a helpless man/woman, they keep the public from knowing why they are attacking him/her. If anybody asks, they lie, and because passers-by don't know what has led to what they see happening, they are left to watch as the blood-thirsty gangs clobber and crush their victim.

Boda-boda gangs do exactly what terrorists do. What do terrorists do? They enter a building, kill people, then change into another set of clothes and raise their hands up, pretending to be victims caught up in the attack. Security personnel sometimes end up helping the terrorists escape from the same mess they have created. That is exactly the same thing that *boda-boda* gangs do. They create a false impression in order to get sympathy from the public. They make the public think that they (gang) have been wronged.

The men who killed my brother kicked his head severally after throwing him to the ground, and stomped on his face with boots that are made for motorcyclists, to be used on rough and rugged terrain. They knocked off his teeth and broke his jaw using a club. They crushed his head using rocks and stones. They did it with so much intensity, it was as if their lives depended on it. They used all manner of crude weapons in their possession or whatever else they could find, to hurt him. They then slashed his head with a machete. They cut away part of his face, then inflicted a deep cut on the back of his head, and another deep cut on top of his head. My brother was left for dead, in unimaginable pain. One of his killers, we are told, emptied his pockets for loose change, then took his wallet and his phone.

My brother was barely alive when members of my family found him, having been alerted about the tragedy by a good-hearted person who witnessed the tragedy but could not leave the area or report it right away for fear of victimization by the killers. Members of my family and this good-hearted person contacted Makongeni Police Station, and they took my brother to the emergency room at the hospital. The doctors assessed the injuries and did all they could to save his life. But my brother had lost too much blood. His life ebbed away.

Beaten, stoned, and slashed with a machete because his government failed him.

How did it fail him?

If the government had weeded out these killers, after the many previous cases in which these same killers maimed and injured innocent members of the public, my brother would not have died. But these criminals were emboldened by the government. They were allowed to terrorize the people of Kiganjo Village without any restraint from government security agencies in Thika District. This is happening across the whole country, wherever *boda-boda* business is happening.

Nevertheless, my late brother's life is not without a memorial. At the spot where he was killed, there are the stones his killers used to kill him. The stones are there as historical markers. They are to be found not far from Kamenu Estate's main entrance, as you come from Kiganjo Village, driving through Makongeni, heading to Thika town. This is just before BAT intersection, off Garissa Road, in Thika.

Those stones proclaim, that Edward died helping others. They proclaim that he was beaten, stoned, slashed with a machete and left for dead. They proclaim that he died a cruel death because his government failed him.

CHAPTER 4

MISSING FILE

"The police are the public and the public are police; the police being only members of the public who are paid to give full time attention to duties which are incumbent on every citizen in the interest of community welfare and existence."
– Robert Peal

There are five things I learnt about Kenya's justice system following the gruesome murder of my brother by a criminal gang.

1. **Rule of Law in Kenya is just a Cliché**

Majority of staff in law enforcement agencies are not interested in seeing justice prevail. The only thing they are interested in is lining their pockets with cash offered to pervert the course of justice.

As earlier indicated, a few days after my brother was killed, my family pleaded with members of the community who had apprehended some of murderers not to harm them. The police were called, and they picked them up. The police officer who was assigned to follow up the case talked to the members of my family at the initial stages, but we later learned that after interrogation, these individuals were allowed to go. My family was not informed, nor were we given any update thereafter. We later learned that an MCA (Member of County Assembly), including the leaders of the *boda-boda* business group and parents of the accused were involved in the illicit arrangements that secured freedom for the murderers. They bribed police officers, who in turn released the killers. Thereafter, all the people in the law enforcement agencies that I talked to, including those at police headquarters, asked for money before they could assist my family. And the amount they asked for was very significant, I must add.

2. No Accountability Whatsoever

My mother and other family members went to the police station in 2016 to get an update, but the officer in charge of the case had nothing for them. My mum requested to talk to the head of the section, and she was accorded the opportunity. The head of the section told her, "I cannot do much to help you because I am not going to be here that long. I am retiring. I have bought land in Eldoret, where I want to spend my retirement."

My mother asked him, "Could you at least start working on it and keep notes of your findings in a file so that whoever comes after you will proceed from where you stopped?"

The head of the section did not do anything. My guess is that as long as it was not a member of his family who had been murdered, he did not feel obligated to do anything.

Let me ask you this: between my mother and the head of the section in that police station, who do you think should have been running the unit? My mother, who did not complete her primary school education, seemed to know more about the process of law than this law enforcement officer.

3. No Consistent and/or Organized Filing System

I went to Thika Police Station for three consecutive days to meet the Assistant to the Head of Criminal Investigations, after flying from the US to Kenya. Do you want to know why I had to go there for three days? The Assistant to the Head of Criminal Investigations at the station had no knowledge of what I was talking about. It did not help that I provided all the information I had about the case. Neither did it help that I was accompanied by family members who had been to the same police station several times to ask of the same thing.

The officer told me, "The file is missing."

I said, "You must be kidding me. How can a whole file of a case as serious as this, just disappear?"

He had no answer, no explanation.

I then asked about the officer who had been assigned to follow up the case.

"He is gone," the head of the department told me.

"Gone where?" I asked.

"He has been transferred."

I asked if we could at least reach out to him to find out if he knew where the file was.

"I hope he didn't go with the file," I said. "If he did, I hope he has not tampered with its contents."

The head of the department promised to reach out to the officer. Several months later, I heard that the file had emerged. But you won't believe where the file was found, even if I told you.

Shockingly, despite all the advance in technology in Kenya, police stations have no effective and reliable method of filing. If you have dealt with law enforcement agencies in Kenya, you know how difficult it is to get any information from them.

4. No Ethics at Work

On one of the days when I was at the police station, meeting with the head of criminal investigations at the branch, I observed a lot of unprofessional conduct. Failure to maintain confidentially hurts victims. For example, if you point out a family seating next to me at a police station and you go ahead and share with me details of their case, in a bid to help me appreciate that there are other people who have suffered the same fate as mine, that family will be hurt, hearing details of their case being narrated to someone who has nothing to do with it.

I appreciate that the officer's intention might have been to show me some empathy by letting me know that he has met other people in my situation, therefore he has an idea of the pain that my brother's death had caused to me and to my family. But it does not come out that way. Instead, it appears like an attempt to minimize the suffering and pain that the families have experienced.

When am at the police station as a victim, I am not there to join a victim support group, where different people who do not know each but have suffered similar situation come together to support each other. I am at a police station to know what the police have done or are doing in regard to the case I'm pursuing. Neither am I at the police station to hear that the file has disappeared. I am at the police station to meet officers who have a duty to perform. That duty entails serving the public. That is why they bear the slogan, *"Utumushi kwa Wote."*

When an injury happens, the suffering and the pain caused by the injury is very much individualized. No amount of comparison or grouping people together who have experienced similar tragedy can lessen the pain they each individually feel.

5. No Truth Allowed

When truth comes out, police react with anger and condemnation, the kind you would expect the police to show when you report crime. But they reserve the anger and turn it on to defend and protect themselves.

One thing though seemed to shake things a little for a day or two before it was quickly silenced. An article about the case was run in one of the national newspapers. The journalist who authored it was summoned by the Officer Commanding Thika Police Station for questioning.

This is what I mean by *"when truth comes out."* The police will do anything to cover up the truth which they already suppressed through the bribes they took from those who want the truth not to come out. If the truth were to come out, the police know that they would be forced to go back and do what they were supposed to have done. That would mean doing what they were asked not to do by those who bribed them in order to hide the truth. Since they already accepted the

When am at the police station as a victim, I am not there to join a victim support group, where different people who do not know each but have suffered similar situation come together to support each other. I am at a police station to know what the police have done or are doing in regard to the case I'm pursuing. Neither am I at the police station to hear that the file has disappeared. I am at the police station to meet officers who have a duty to perform. That duty entails serving the public.

bribe and soiled their hands, they must remain soiled all the way. The police know that those who bribed them can blackmail them, that's why they (police) hide the truth in order to protect the interests of those who bribed them. Threats, intimidation, harassment or even death are used to silence both those who know the truth, and those seeking the truth.

That is what is happening to my brother's case.

CHAPTER 5

FAILURE OF THE GOVERNMENT

"Worse than a corrupt government is an incompetent one, not least because having the second characteristic does not exclude the first one." - Victor Bello Accioly

I was embarrassed by the quality of service that Kenyans receive at our police stations. It is poor, to say the least. But it is not just at police stations. The government has made colossal mistakes that have caused millions of Kenyan families untold suffering and agony. The government has created, allowed and promoted an unsafe environment.

Take the case of *boda-boda* gangs, like the one that murdered my brother. The government through the judicial system determines the procedures through which the criminals are to be arrested, sentenced, and punished. The government also allocates the budget for the police work. So, it's important that the government gives enough resources to the judicial agencies to make sure they are well equipped for the work of putting away the criminal elements.

There is no doubt that fear of retaliation by *boda-boda* riders kept the three people who were with my brother from revealing the identity of the murderers to the police. If members of the public had confidence in the police, prosecutors and judges, that criminals who get arrested would not escape justice, they would tip the police about criminals in their midst without fear of retaliation. If members of the public know that criminals, when apprehended, get the justice they deserve, they will fearlessly volunteer information to police officers that will lead to the arrest of the criminals. But if members of the public find that the criminals merely get a slap on the hand for heinous crimes, because the judicial system is compromised, they will not cooperate with the police.

Whenever and wherever crime happens, community members are assumed to be less willing to cooperate with law enforcement officers if penalties meted are seen to be too low. Members of the public regard it as a waste of their time in addition to exposing them to danger in the event that word leaks out about who reported the activities of the gang members to the police.

This brings me to something that really concerned me when I visited Thika police station. It was very unclear to me when talking to officers at the police station whose responsibility it was to charge my brother's murderers, or even who was responsible to do what. Forgive my ignorance of the court procedure and processes in Kenya, but I don't understand how the police can arrest someone after members of the public apprehended him for committing murder, and then let him go scot free without preferring any charges against him.

How do you send back to the community criminals that were handed over to you by members of the same community? You send them back to the community that has been hurt, the community that is willing to help with the case by bringing forth witnesses and evidence of crime committed.

One big problem with the police in Kenya, is that instead of following the laid down judicial process to deal with law breakers, they set up their own Kangaroo courts where they act as the investigator, prosecutor and judge. And as one would expect, no records are availed to show what happened, or what was done.

What is a Kangaroo court?

A kangaroo court is a "court" that ignores recognized standards of law or justice, and often carries little or no official standing in the territory within which it resides. The term may also apply to a court held by a legitimate judicial authority who intentionally disregards the court's legal or ethical obligations.

Source: Wikipedia

It is the work of the police to arrest, then file charges and allow prosecution to take its course. One of the greatest contributions by the police in the fight against crime is to deter crime by increasing the perception that criminals will be caught and punished.

The police deter crime when they do things that strengthen a criminal's perception that chances of getting caught are very high. Strategies that police could use as "sentinels," such as hot spots policing, are particularly effective. A criminal's behavior is more likely to be impacted by seeing a police officer with handcuffs and a radio than by a new law that increases penalties. The certainty of being caught is a vastly more powerful deterrent than the punishment.

Courthouse

The court sets and approves bail. This is to allow a person who has been charged to remain free until found guilty or not guilty. This allows the accused person to continue coming to court for hearings related to the charges filed against him/her as opposed to keeping him/her in jail until the case is over. Eventually, if the person charged is found guilty of the crime or crimes he/she is charged with, he/she gets sentenced.

When a police officer arrests someone for murder or any other crime and places them in remand, and then lets them go after receiving a bribe, that police officer violates all the rules that lead to justice. That police officer has taken a role that is more than that assigned to a police officer. Such an officer assumes the role of a prosecutor and a judge at the same time. I would even say that they have even assumed the role of a warden. Such an officer is unworthy to be a custodian of the law.

The sentence is declared by a judge, which can be that you pay a fine, or do community service, or be placed on probation, or be sent to prison, or any other sentence the judge deems appropriate, including paying for restitution. This is what is called punishment for crimes committed. It is only rendered by a court of law.

As indicated above, a judge can decide to send a criminal to prison. That is part of the judicial system. Prison is part of the criminal justice system, or correction system. A court sends criminals to prison for rehabilitation. Rehabilitation is a central goal of the correctional system. This goal rests on the assumption that individuals can be rehabilitated and can return to a crime-free life.

Justice System

People whose rights have been violated deserve justice. Those who violate those rights, meaning those charged and found guilty receive what is just for them. This is meant to help those who were violated feel that something has been done to mitigate their pain and suffering, and the violation of their rights.

The court and the prison system, working together with the police, are mandated to do this work to serve the public. They are not supposed to use the system to enrich themselves.

Prosecutor

There is a very important person in a court-room – the prosecutor. The prosecutor's role is to bring charges (prosecution) against those charged with crimes. The prosecutor mentions the charges at the start of the proceedings, with the judge present and the accused too. The accused is one who has been charged but not yet sentenced.

The prosecutor represents the country and bring the charges against the accused on behalf of the city or the country. It's a way of saying, *the laws of the land have been violated or broken.* The crimes committed have violated not just the rights of the person who is aggrieved, but the whole country. To be specific, the crimes have been committed against the people in the district where the court that adjudicates the case is located. The laws that have been broken are explained by the prosecutor, who also suggests the appropriate punishment. It is the role of the prosecutor to vigorously defend those laws.

If the prosecutor or prosecution fails in its work, it's the government that has failed to ensure justice for its people. And if the judge fails to render sound judgment, the whole judicial system is deemed to have failed. So, one judge can taint the name of the whole judicial system by allowing himself/herself to be influenced by outside forces in deciding a particular case.

The prosecution and the judge are two different offices, but they work together as a team to clean the house, so to say. In deciding cases, passing judgment and sentencing, judges are supposed to follow sentencing guidelines. They are not supposed to follow what their loved ones or friends tell them.

From the time the charges are read in court for the first time to the time when sentencing is done, there is room for arguments about what happened, and who did what. This is also the time when witnesses are called. It is important to point out that police are part of witnesses. These are some of the tools that a prosecutor has at his/her disposal when prosecuting any case. A police officer needs to be in court to give a testimony in regard to the arrest they made, and why they made the arrest. They are also supposed to identify the person they arrested, who is supposed to be present in court. In addition, the prosecution is at liberty to produce any other evidence to strengthen its case.

The judge hears the charges and listens to the response made by the accused or his/her lawyer. The judge then decides to either allow bail or deny it.

I am sure you sense my concern.

When a police officer arrests someone for murder or any other crime and places them in remand, and then lets them go after receiving a bribe, that police officer violates all the rules that lead to justice. That police officer has taken a role that is more than that assigned to a police officer. Such an officer assumes the role of a prosecutor and a judge at the same time. I would even say that they have even assumed the role of a warden. Such an officer is unworthy to be a custodian of the law.

Majority of the police officers we have in Kenya have put a dent on the judicial system by keeping those who deserve to be sentenced from being sentenced. Instead, they allow the criminals, who don't deserve to be in the society, to roam free. There is a place for the criminals. They have chosen, by their behavior, to go to that place. But the police keep them from going where they deserve to go. They do this by receiving bribes from the criminals.

When police officers short-circuit prison punishment by receiving bribes, they abandon the duty they vowed to uphold, which makes them worse than the criminals themselves. Such police officers are not worthy of their title. They are not worth the badge they wear. They are the scum of the earth. They make the public lose by allowing criminals who should not be free enjoy unmerited freedom.

There is a second reason why members of the public tell me of what is happening where they live. They tell me they report to me because they can't report to the government anymore. Why? Because they have no faith in the government. They tell me that the government is unable to protect even its own staff.

These criminals are a danger to society. What they need is rehabilitation, not freedom. Now, rehabilitation happens in prison, not in the streets or at home. So, when police officers allow criminals to go back home, or to our streets, they do the society a big disfavor. As a matter of fact, they are putting the lives of many in danger. My brother is not here to tell you this, but I have a number of victims who have been maimed by members of *boda-boda* gangs who can testify that what I am sharing here is true.

My brother's death is proof of that. Those who killed him had assaulted other people before, but the police turned a blind eye to their evil deeds. Knowing that nothing will happen to them, the murderers descended on my brother, not just to maim him, but to kill him, which they did. These horrendous evils have their genesis in failure by the whole government structure to perform its duty.

As I write, I just received information that *boda-boda* riders in

Kiganjo threatened another man. They sent a message that they want him, and they want him harmed. What more do police need to act? Isn't that enough? The family called me to let me know. Why did they call me, you ask? They called me because I care. They called me because I have been there. I have seen what these criminals can do. They killed my brother. I am having to bear the pain of the loss of my brother every waking day of my life.

I have a question for judges in Kenya; why have you forfeited your power and mandate to the police? Maybe I should ask it this way: does it bother you that the police have hijacked your offices and assumed your power altogether?

What this means, is that the criminals that need to be prosecuted and judged in Kenya before all others are police officers. Why? Because they are thieves. They have stolen positions that don't belong to them. They are exercising power that isn't theirs.

Another question for judges and prosecutors; how do you sleep at night, knowing that majority of all those arrested for crimes shall not see the corridors of the court-room, leave alone the inside of it?

There is a second reason why members of the public tell me of what is happening where they live. They tell me they report to me because they can't report to the government anymore. Why? Because they have no faith in the government. They tell me that the government is unable to protect even its own staff.

They tell me that their chief, a government officer, walks with a limp, which resulted from an attack by a *boda-boda* gang. Can you believe that? Criminals attacked a chief and nothing happened to them! And so, the public says, *if the government cannot protect its staff from these criminals, there is nothing it can do to protect us.*

Listening to members of the public talk like that, you really can't blame them for feeling helpless. This will continue unless huge change takes place.

What should we as citizens do?

I want to know your thoughts on these questions and others that are forming in your mind as you read this. Share with others in our Facebook forum, www.facebook.com/yourspeakout

You will find what other people have to say about this grievous concern. You can also join our *speak out speak up for a life* community on our website: www.speakoutspeakup.life

CHAPTER 6

CONDITION OF THE COUNTRY

"A government is corrupt when it is strictly profit-driven, not driven to serve the best interests of its people."
– Suzy Kassem

Kenyans are paying dearly for failing to make a break with bad leaders. Our dalliance with bad leaders has led to the loss of lives of many Kenyans and destroyed the future of our children.

We have been fooled over and over again to believe the empty promises given by our leaders. And you can't entirely blame the leaders. George Orwell correctly opined, that *a people that elect corrupt politicians, imposters, thieves and traitors are not victims but accomplices.*

The Dark Side that Rules Kenya

What I share here is just a tip of the iceberg. There is a much larger dark side that is not seen or known. It might also be that people are not interested to know. That might explain why things are as they are today in our country.

Bad leaders take pleasure in knowing that their people are not interested in knowing the root cause of the many ills they suffer. This lack of knowledge on the side of the public benefits bad leaders, who deliberately scheme to ensure that the public remains in the dark. This lack of interest to know is a recipe for disaster.

Who experiences the disaster?

The public does. You and I and our children experience the disaster that our leaders have helped to create.

My brother had many visible injuries when he was rushed to the hospital. But there were injuries that were not visible until a thorough assessment was done. In the same way, there is a lot that you don't see when you look around in our country, but so much bad has been done and continues unabated.

Kenyans experience myriads of problems daily, but they don't know what causes them. The government has failed in its responsibilities. This current government has had more chances and more resources to make a positive change, but instead of putting them into good use, all the resources are ending up in the pockets of our leaders. Kenyans are willing to partner with the government in building their country, but this government is wasting all those chances. It is dashing the hope of its citizens.

In Kenya, when your rights have been violated, and you go to the police to seek justice, do you know what the police do? They respond by asking you to bribe them so they can pursue those who violated your rights. How can the police, who are the custodians of the law, ask you to bribe them so they can do their work?

This can only happen in a country that is run by gangs of thugs and criminals. And that is what we have in Kenya.

When struggling to figure out why the police were not making any progress in the case involving the murder of my brother, I was given the contact of a very senior person at police headquarters. I got the contact from a well-connected person in the corridors of power.

I couldn't bring myself to believe what I heard when I contacted the senior person at police headquarters. I am going to paraphrase what the senior police officer told me: "I always knew there will be difficulties in bringing to justice those who killed Edward. This is because there are a number of people who are senior than me who are protecting the murderers. I can lose my job if I make a move to help you. But if you are willing to provide funds so that I get all I need to get all the murderers arrested, I will work with you."

Can you believe that?

My brother has been murdered, and the government officials who are supposed to enforce justice, are blocking it. And not only that, they are ready to profit from our misfortune.

I had asked a simple question: why was there no progress in

the case, when criminals who had murdered my brother had been identified? All I needed was some feedback. Or an update. The response by the senior police officer sounded like an appeal for me to fund a war! It was as if the government official wanted me to sponsor the take-over of another country. You know, if they are going to take over another country, they need heavy equipment. They need war planes. If I'm asking for this war to take place, then I'm obligated to fund it. It's my responsibility to provide funds for what is needed to carry it through. If they need a warship to complete the mission, I better be prepared financially.

What a mess!

You don't find this in a country whose leaders are serious about the safety of their people.

We know from research that high level of patrol and monitoring by law enforcement encourages willingness by members of the public to cooperate with the police. If the public sees the police regularly in risky and dangerous zones, they see them as their allies in fighting crime. The public is smart. People can tell where law enforcement is investing its time, energy and resources.

In Kenya, police do not focus on areas where crime is more likely to happen. Instead, they focus on instances where they can treat the public like ATM machines and get as much as they can in form of bribes. If those getting hurt, maimed and killed can't serve as ATM

> *It was as if the government official wanted me to sponsor the take-over of another country. You know, if they are going to take over another country, they need heavy equipment. They need war planes. If I'm asking for this war to take place, then I'm obligated to fund it. It's my responsibility to provide funds for what is needed to carry it through. If they need a warship to complete the mission, I better be prepared financially.*

machines, they are left on their own.

My brother was killed just a few feet from a police station at Makongeni, in Thika. Isn't that a big shame? The thugs have neither respect nor fear of the police. This is proof of the evil collaboration between *boda-boda* gangs and the police. The criminals don't even fear to murder a human being not far from a police station.

Police officers at Makongeni Police Station did not act or do anything in terms of making arrests or opening a file after they were informed of the attack. They were informed of what had happened and who had caused it. They came and picked my brother like they were picking a dead person's body even though he wasn't yet dead. I wonder if it crossed their mind that what had happened could have been avoided if they, the police, had acted differently? Why did they not show up sooner? Where were they? What were they doing that was more important than public safety?

Boda-boda gangs have compromised the police. No wonder they are not afraid to kill near a police station. No wonder the police don't pursue cases of those who have been hurt, maimed or killed by *boda-boda* riders. I have talked to individuals who have been injured or maimed and also to their family members and I can report that they don't know what to do. They live in agony and fear day-in-day-out. What has happened to them or to their loved ones is a shame, given that they live in a country that has a government – if really there is a government.

The *boda-boda* gangs give money to the police so they can look the other way and leave the gangs to rule the roads and the neighborhoods the way they want. The money the gangs pay guarantees that their members will not face any charges irrespective of the crime(s) they commit. This, in the end, translates to the victim not receiving justice through the court system.

Politicians Benefit from this Lawless Group

I pointed out earlier that politicians use members of *boda-boda* gangs during election time to do their dirty work. They are used to create havoc and confusion and to punish, destroy, demoralize and kill those who dare challenge or oppose the paymaster of the gangs.

It is for this reason that politicians will not do anything to eradicate the environment that allows these gangs to flourish. The former MCA of Kamenu Ward in Kiganjo, where my brother was killed is reported as among those who protected the *boda-boda* riders who killed my brother.

Connections between politicians and the *boda-boda* riders begin to form from the time politicians who solicit their services begin to campaign for public offices. Then the gangs move on to work for the politicians when they get elected. This to me is election by intimidation. When you have members of a group that is terrorizing the public on the campaign trail and in public offices, what are you as a leader telling the public? It shows that our leaders have no problem with the actions of these lawless groups.

This is how *boda-boda* gangs acquire protection.

Many of our elected leaders use *boda-boda* gangs to help them get elected. What does that tell you about the mindset of our leaders? It should come as no surprise that when our leaders assume office, they treat the public the same way. The only difference is that their violation of the public is not obvious to the undiscerning. But the violations committed by politicians are same as those committed by the gangs. Our leaders do this in the public offices they occupy. They don't do what we send them to those public offices to do. If they did, we would not be talking about the things we are talking about here, because we would be having a better country than we have now. The question is, why do we keep electing the same brand of politicians again and again?

I support and call for removal of all leaders who entertain and allow criminal activities by *boda-boda* gangs. It's obvious that the gangs would want these leaders to continue in office, to guarantee their protection. But the public should be vigilant and demand that they resign right away.

PART 2

TRUE AND GENUINE FRIENDSHIP

"The sincere friends of this world are as a ship lights in the stormiest of nights." – Anthony J. Angelo

The reason I included this section is because it seems – at least to me – like most of us have lost the art of friendship, or what true and genuine friendship entails.

Looking back and thinking hard about the tragedy that hit our family, I cannot help but think of ways I can remind everyone what true and genuine friendship really means.

I have not seen any record or heard of any efforts by the three people who were with my brother the night he was killed, to save his life.

That's really scary, if you ask me.

CHAPTER 7

CONDITION OF THE SOCIETY

"We cannot rely on anyone else in the world to take charge of our community and our society. That's on us."
– Joe Mungai

It's true our leaders have failed us, but we have also failed ourselves. One can tell this by looking at the margin by which we have allowed our leaders to fail us. Let me show you what failing ourselves entails.

As a society we have lost our focus. We have lost our equilibrium. We have failed to take charge of our communities. Consequently, we have failed to care for each other. We have lost the sense of protecting our neighbors. We walk away from a fellow human being who desperately needs our help and feel nothing about it. It does not matter whether the cry for help is coming from someone who is right before our eyes, or from another part of the country. We simply are not interested. Corrupt government officials and evil gangs benefit from such an attitude by members of the public. They like such an environment, because they know that they can do what they want without restraint by the public. And so, ours has been exploited to the maximum.

The three people who were with my brother walked away when he was attacked. They went their merry way, leaving a fellow human being behind being butchered like an animal. They walked away without trying to get people to come and help. They walked away without letting the authorities know what was happening. They walked away and went home to their safety, leaving my brother all alone to be killed. They walked away and went to sleep, knowing very well that a fellow human being was being killed.

How could they go to sleep, given what they had witnessed?

If they could sleep through that, then you know that we have a big problem in our country.

When you walk away to safety and leave others in unsafe places or in need of your help, how do you live with that consciousness? As a society what is our condition? Why does a community accept to be run over by a group of gangsters?

I'll admit that, I have struggled a lot to understand this phenomenon. It's an aspect of the discussion to which we shall return.

However, I don't write this to heap up criticism against the three friends or members of Kiganjo community, because what happened there is typical of what is happening across the whole country. You could just as well erase *Kiganjo* or *Thika* and put *Nakuru, Mombasa,* or *Eldoret* in its place. We would be extremely short-sighted if we thought our particular town or village makes us immune to this crisis that is tearing communities apart. Rather, this critical situation – a story that's been told again and again – is common to every village and town, no matter your circumstances right now.

Taking Action

Let's talk about taking action to improve the current condition of our lives. If we don't take action, no one else will. That's the hard truth. Everyone in Kenya should know that, because it's pretty obvious. But the reality of what I see and hear tells me that majority of our people don't appreciate that. Otherwise, why are we doing nothing to improve the quality of our lives? Or to improve our safety? Or even to demand better services from the government of the day?

Make no mistake; no one will come to do these things for us. When those we expect to change the condition of our country come and see the state we are in, instead of helping us to improve, they will call us stupid.

You know who a stupid person is?

Here it is:

Definition of Stupid:

Knowing The Truth, Seeing The Truth, Still Believing the Lies.

Source: Inspirational quote guru

Here is the truth; no one will come to fix what needs to be fixed in Kenya. Only Kenyans will. If we want to live like animals, it's up to us. If we want to change the negative conditions in our country, that is also up to us.

It is foolhardy to rely on anyone else in the world to take charge of our community and our country. Everyone else is busy taking charge of their own community and their own country. And so, if you are waiting – you are going to wait for a very long time.

The Future of Our Children

What do we tell our children when we raise them in an environment that is vile and horrible, when we have the power to change it, but we don't? Is that not creating a recipe for disaster for all future generations?

When you model this lifestyle to your children, you are in effect telling them, *this is the acceptable way for humans to live.* But which humans? Because not all humans live that way or encourage and promote that kind of a lifestyle. Not all humans model that kind of a lifestyle to their children.

What are we teaching our children to do tomorrow? Because mark my words; they will do the same things they see you doing today. This means your grandchildren will be raised in the same horrible conditions that you have helped to create. They will live in the same conditions you have allowed to thrive. We all must be constantly aware of the fact that we cannot rely on anyone else in the world to take charge of our community and our country. That's on us!

Demand Different Conditions

New and different conditions might spare someone's life.

The truth is, that you don't know who the criminal gangs will kill next in your community. It might be a member of your family. If you wait longer, it might be too late. I'm inviting you to take some of my courage and make it yours. The courage you have always wanted but you didn't have. The courage to tell your leaders that enough is enough.

What happened to being our brother's keeper? We are reminded not to withhold good from those who deserve it, when it is in our power to act (Proverbs 3:27).

In the animal kingdom, animals knows how to protect each other and help each other during times of need. All you need to do to witness this reality is turn on to a wildlife channel on your TV set. But I guess you already know that. Why, then, don't we do what we know to be the right thing to do?

As a people, what have we become?

The Three Friends

Can you imagine just how Edward must have been frightened out of his mind when he saw his friends walk away from him instead of forming a shield around him, or at least talk sense to the marauding thugs to restrain them? They chose to walk away and not look back.

It is foolhardy to rely on anyone else in the world to take charge of our community and our country. Everyone else is busy taking charge of their own community and their own country. And so, if you are waiting – you are going to wait for a very long time.

They heard my brother scream for help, but they did nothing to help him.

How could they leave him? They were the only people who knew the truth of the matter. How could they leave him when he was screaming for their help?

As he watched them walk away, he must have hoped that they would reach down into their human conscience and at least attempt to get him some help. He must have remained hopeful even as he was being brutally beaten that some help would come eventually. But it never did. His friends did not have what it takes to help another human being. They could have told the killers, *we know him, please don't hurt him. And if you are going hurt him, hurt us too.* But they didn't. And most likely, as soon as he was out of their sight, he was out of their mind.

The People on the Road

Imagine how Edward hoped that those driving and walking on the same road would stop and help him. But none of them did. He screamed for their help and asked them to intervene. But none of them responded. None of them came close. They all stayed on the periphery. No one dared to step into the ring to be counted as different from the rest. They chose instead to stand in stunned silence and witness a tragedy that need not have happened. It was as though those who knew what was about to happen were just waiting to see how it would happen. They did not make any attempt to rescue my brother. They did nothing to stop an innocent life from being snuffed out.

The People in that Neighborhood

Edward must have hoped that the people in Phase 5 who heard him scream for help and those who looked through their windows would respond and do something to help him. But rather than help him, they chose to remain in their warm houses and do nothing to help him at that moment when he most needed them.

The People Who Killed Him

Edward must have hoped that his killers would take time to meditate on how he had spared their lives by not running over them. This he did by attempting to reach the police station from another road rather than plow through the second group of *boda-boda* riders who were coming from BAT and had parked in the road to block him from driving through. This second group had been contacted by the first group, which had pursued him from Kiganjo to Makongeni.

The Police Officers

Edward must have hoped that police officers at Makongeni who had been informed of the whole incident (by someone who watched the whole ordeal but waited until the killers had left before walking to the scene) would act right away and make arrests. But the police did not act right away. All they did was take Edward away and the person who had reported, together with my family members, to the hospital. That was the last time we heard of them.

CHAPTER 8

WHAT DOES TRUE FRIENDSHIP LOOK LIKE?

"True friends aren't the ones who make your problems disappear. They are the ones who won't disappear when you are facing problems."
– Soitsbeensaid.tumblr

We can learn a lot about genuine friendship by observing friendships throughout Scripture.

In particular, we will look at the friendship that existed between Jonathan and David as a resource to help us appreciate what most of us seem to have forgotten – what true friendship looks like. We all need to understand that friends put plans into place to save their friends out of danger when it becomes necessary to do so, however high the cost might be. That is what we see Jonathan doing for David at a very great cost to himself.

The friendship between David and Jonathan shows us three truths which help us understand the nature of true friendship.

This resource was edited by Scott Slayton who serves as Lead Pastor at Chelsea Village Baptist Church. It originated from crosswalk.com, an online Christian living resource platform.

3 Truths about Genuine Friendship that We Can Learn from David and Jonathan

1. Friendship Springs from a Strong Bond

After the Lord rejected Jonathan's father as king, the prophet Samuel anointed David, but in 1 Samuel 18, the formal transfer of power was yet to take place. After David defeated Goliath, Saul grew jealous of David because the people sang that Saul killed thousands, but David had killed tens of thousands. Nevertheless, David met Saul's family and forged a tight-knit friendship with Jonathan.

As soon as he had finished speaking to Saul, the soul of Jonathan was knit to the soul of David, and Jonathan loved him as his own soul. And Saul took him that day and would not let him return to his father's house. Then Jonathan made a covenant with David, because he loved him as his own soul. And Jonathan stripped himself of the robe that was on him and gave it to David, and his armor, and even his sword and his bow and his belt. And David went out and was successful wherever Saul sent him, so that Saul set him over the men of war. And this was good in the sight of all the people and also in the sight of Saul's servants (1 Samuel 18:1-5).

All of the language the writer of 1 Samuel uses suggests a strong bond between David and Jonathan. He says their souls were "knit" together and that Jonathan loved David "as his own soul. Then Jonathan made a covenant with David and demonstrated the reality of his promise by giving his robe, armor, and weapons to David.

A covenant is so much more than a contract. Covenant is rooted in promise and relationship. It implies a bond that cannot be broken except by death. This becomes especially clear when we consider that the covenant Christians enjoy with God was bound by the blood of His Son. Christians are adopted as the sons of God through faith in Jesus Christ who loved us and gave Himself up for us.

We are brothers and sisters. We are a family. Think about the language used to describe the church – a family, a building, and a body. Do you see the interconnectedness in each of those metaphors? If the church is a temple, then we are bricks in it. If the church is a body, we are its members. If the church is a family, we have a place at the table. Therefore, Christians have every reason to pursue real and vital friendships because we share so much in common. C.S. Lewis said friendship begins when one person says to another, "What? You too? I thought no one but myself."

2. Friendship Shares a Mutual Affection

One of the foundations of a strong friendship is a shared affection and love for one another. Jonathan and David's friendship demonstrates this, as evidenced by the language used to describe it.

We don't spend very much time thinking about the nature of true friendship. In our social-media dominated age, we are so image-conscious that we think more about the impression that we make than we do about making genuine friends. If you are not careful, you will carefully craft an image using social media and not allow people to get too close because it would ruin the image. Then, you build your identity on the number of people who are impressed by you and who respond to the image you have created.

You have an important choice to make – you can impress people or you can have genuine friends. When we develop real friendships, our friends will know we are not that impressive. They will see the rough edges and the ugliest things about us, but we will be known and we will be loved. That is the beauty of true friendship – it sees the ugly and it stays.

You have an important choice to make – you can impress people or you can have genuine friends. When we develop real friendships, our friends will know we are not that impressive. They will see the rough edges and the ugliest things about us, but we will be known and we will be loved. That is the beauty of true friendship – it sees the ugly and it stays.

The root of all genuine friendship is God's love toward us. God's love toward us has nothing to do with our being impressive enough for Him to love. When we read the Bible we see quite the opposite, don't we? "But God demonstrated his own love toward us, in that while we were still sinners Christ died for us." God showed His love in giving us the greatest gift we could receive when we were not impressive. In fact, He knows us deeper than we could be known and loves more than we could ever be loved. What blows me away about God is He says to us, "I know everything about you and I love you deeply."

God's love for us in Christ model's genuine friendship for us. We are too quick to run from friendships because they seem too difficult or feel like too much trouble. Yet, Christ went through the pain and the difficulty of the cross for us. How can we not take the hard road in our friendships with other believers? This means overlooking personality quirks, forgiving when you are wronged, and walking with others through difficulty, but to walk through life with genuine friends is worth every pain and effort we put into it.

3. Friendship Demands Selfless Sacrifice

When Jonathan stripped off his armor and weapons, he told us a lot about how he thinks things are going to go between he and David. Jonathan's gift acknowledged that David will be king instead of him and instead of his father.

Then Jonathan went the extra mile for David. When he discovered that his father planned to kill David, he put a plan in place to save David at great cost to himself. He sent David away to hide while he sought to gauge the depth of his father's anger towards David.

When David did not show up to dinner for a second night, Jonathan told his father that he allowed David to go to a feast. Saul responded by insulting his son and calling for David to be put to death. Jonathan asked his father why he wanted to kill David and Saul responded by throwing a spear at him. At this point, the writer of 1 Samuel made an astute observation. *"So, Jonathan knew that his father was determined to put David to death."*

The next morning, Jonathan went out into the field and was able to tell David about his father's murderous plans. The two shared an emotional farewell and David fled from Saul. Jonathan's care for David shows us something of the sacrifice involved in friendship. He was loyal to his bond to protect David even though it meant he would not get to be king. He did this at great cost and danger to himself. His father cursed him and threw a spear at him. He could have died as a result of his father's rage, but he stayed the course because he made a promise to his friend.

Friendship necessarily entails sacrifice. A friendship cannot survive for long if each person involved tends to be self-centered and is unable to put aside their own preferences for the sake of others. The traits that make a friendship flourish involve sacrifice because a genuine friendship involves sacrificing time, resources, emotional energy, and preferences. It means getting to know people, making time to spend with them, bearing with their failures, and working to forgive them when they wrong us.

The beauty of sacrifice in friendship is that it leads to great joy. Jesus said the person who loses his life will find it and the one who saves his life will lose it. Jesus endured the cross *"for the joy set before him."* These are the surprising values of God's kingdom. Joy comes through pouring ourselves out for others. Real pleasure comes from having less of our lives revolve around ourselves. The world says to focus only on yourself, but Jesus shows us that life is lived wrongly if we live it only for ourselves.

If you struggle to know how to be a friend, look at your Savior. He said greater love has no one than this that someone would lay down his life for a friend. He could say this was the mark of a true friend because this is exactly what He was about to do for His disciples and for us. Jesus gave Himself for us. May this guide the way we approach all of our friendships.

PART 3

TWO CHALLENGES
KENYANS FACE TODAY

The first one comes from leaders who treat Kenyans as an option.

The second challenge comes from members of *boda-boda* gangs that harass and oppress Kenyans ruthlessly.

I don't think Kenyans are adequately warned about these two dangers. I consider it imperative for all Kenyans to be fully informed.

Let's turn our focus on these two challenges.

CHAPTER 9

THE GOVERNMENT TREATS KENYANS AS AN OPTION

"Government is the servant, not the master."
- Abhijit Naskar

I will introduce this chapter by sending a message to all Kenyan citizens:

When your government treats you like an option (which it does), help it narrow its choices by removing yourself from the equation.

If you don't, you have already signed your own death warrant. And not only yours, but also that of your children and your children's children.

Let's dive in together and consider the subject at hand.

I want to give you ten examples of what it means to be treated as an option by our leaders. But before I do, I want to let you know how you can help your government change by removing yourself from this equation that regards you as an option.

There are two ways you can do that.

1. Vote These Leaders Out

In other words, vote in new leaders who are committed to serving those who put them into public office. Vote for a leader who will treat you right.

Voting is your right. You can use it to change the relationship you have with your leaders for better or for worse. You can change it for better by voting in new leaders who respect the rule of law, or change it for worse by voting in the same leaders who are evil and corrupt.

When citizens of other countries talk about democracy, they typically emphasize the importance of the right to vote. They understand that you can impact the future of your children by the leaders you vote in today.

Election Day should be a holiday as citizens celebrate the day they exercise their power against tyrannical leaders of their day.

The right to vote has always been on shaky ground in Kenya as it has been in many other African countries.

How is that?

In Kenya, we allow ourselves to be manipulated into electing leaders we do not necessarily resonate with. It has been said that in Kenya, during an election, a slogan is all Kenyans need to vote in their leaders. They are not interested in policies, no blueprint detailing what those aspiring for office will aim to accomplish. All they need is a slogan that tickles them.

For how long shall we allow this to continue? For how long shall we remain a laughing stock in the eyes of other nations? How much longer shall we be seen as a pathetic people who never learn? How much longer do we want to continue leaving in our man-made prisons when we have the power (vote) to unlock them?

2. Protest and Express Disgust at Bad Treatment from the Government

I want to be very clear: protest here does not mean violence or violation of the law. It does not mean destroying property or hurting people. If you violate the law, you defeat the whole purpose of your protest. Citizens who violate the law when protesting are no better than the government they are trying to change.

Not too long ago, residents of Marsabit offered dirty drinking water to their leaders, who had failed to provide them with clean drinking water. That was a good, effective protest.

Professor Wangari Maathai was very good at organizing and coordinating protests. We owe her a lot for all she did to protect our public places from being grabbed by corrupt politicians.

You have a right to speak out any time, wherever you are. But there are many questions that come into play when you decide to organize a protest. When do you need a police permit? Are there things you cannot say or do? Are there any limitations as to when or where you can demonstrate? What about civil disobedience?

Know Your Rights: Free Speech, Protests & Demonstrations
Members of American Civil Rights Union (ACLU) have helpful information which I have modified for our consumption.

This guide outlines your free-speech rights and the steps you can take to keep your demonstration lawful. It defines the limits to your rights, including when speech may not be protected; and what you can expect if you engage in civil disobedience. It gives you the tools to recognize when your rights have been violated.

Key DOs & DON'Ts of Demonstrating
Conduct, Not Content: Your right to express your opinion is protected no matter what beliefs you hold.

Free-speech rights are for everybody. It doesn't matter whether you're a Kenyan citizen, whether you're of voting age, or whether you speak English or not. You have a right to free speech.

When, Where, and How: Every city has regulations. It's your responsibility to understand them.

Don't have a permit?

You can: Hold a small rally in a public park or march on the sidewalk and obey traffic laws.

Stop willing passersby to hand them a leaflet, engage them in conversation, or ask them to sign a petition.

Register people to vote in shopping malls or other public venues.

You **DON'T** have the right to engage in free-speech activity on private property. Shopping malls are an exception. (Private walkways and parking lots in front of some malls or free-standing stores like Tuskys in Kenya or Target in US are not part of this exception).

There are different rules for different locations. Make sure you look up local laws. Be aware that laws vary from city to city.

How to Get a Permit

The government cannot prohibit marches on public sidewalks or streets, or rallies in most public parks or plazas. However, it can require a permit.

Permit ordinances should require advance notice of a protest measured in days, not weeks, and there should be an exception to allow demonstrations in response to breaking news.

Cities can't:

Reroute your march away from busy crowds or main streets or dictate when it must start and end – because you can't communicate your message if nobody can hear it;

Deny a permit just because past demonstrations by your group or others ended in civil disobedience;

Charge increased fees because the content of the event is controversial;

Charge burdensome fees, but they can charge for the costs of processing permits.

Protected Speech

As long as your words don't directly incite violence or law-breaking, you cannot be held responsible for the way that counter demonstrators or your own supporters react.

Your right to free speech **DOES NOT** extend to libel, slander, obscenity, "true threats," or speech that incites imminent violence or law-breaking. If you grab a megaphone during a protest and yell "shoot the cop," or "loot the shop," your speech is **NOT** protected.

Campuses & Clinics = LIMITS

You cannot physically obstruct or intentionally interfere with the staff, patients, or building of a medical clinic offering reproductive health services. This also applies to houses of worship.

You **CAN** organize a protest at your public school or university, but the school may require you to observe reasonable time, place and manner regulations, including not interfering with class.

Civil Disobedience & Arrest

Civil disobedience is the active refusal to comply with certain laws as a form of protest. If you're planning to block an intersection or chain yourself to a building:

Keep a valid ID and a list of phone numbers on your person. You may request an attorney and make up to three local phone calls if you are arrested.

Be aware of consequences particular to you before engaging in civil disobedience. For example, if you are a non-citizen, an arrest may affect your immigration status.

Restrictions on Police

Police officers may not use their powers in a way that has a "chilling effect" on ordinary people who wish to express their views. However, they can break up acts of civil disobedience or gatherings no longer observing reasonable time, place and manner restrictions.

You have the right to film the police.

In public spaces, you **CAN** photograph or film the police and police activity.

You have a right to speak out any time, wherever you are. But there are many questions that come into play when you decide to organize a protest. When do you need a police permit? Are there things you cannot say or do? Are there any limitations as to when or where you can demonstrate? What about civil disobedience?

The police **CANNOT** demand to view your photographs or video without a warrant, but they may be able to seize your phone while they get one. They should return it (or a copy of your data) within a few days. The police **CANNOT** delete your images.

The police may order you to cease activities that interfere with law enforcement. In private spaces, the owner can limit photos.

NOTE: The police can also photograph or videotape events that are open to the public, including protests. However, citizens' right to privacy prohibits maintaining unnecessary information.

Even though you have a constitutional right to film, you can't interfere in an investigation, and you might be hassled if you appear to be doing so.

Now let's look at the 10 ways your leaders treat you as an option. This way, you can figure out what to do about it.

10 Signs Your Government Is Treating You Like An Option

Your relationship with your government is very much like a relationship between two people who are in a healthy relationship.

In a two-people relationship, the way your partner treats you, or you treat them, according to Steven Altchison whose article I adopted for this conversation, will be "the make or break of your happiness." Yes, we seek happiness from inside, but you shouldn't have to dig deeper because your partner is making you miserable or mistreating you, says Steven. He adds: "In all of our relationships, respect should be first and foremost."

But how do we know if we are being treated like an option by our government leaders? Things seem to be going ok. We do recognize some signs, but for the most part, these leaders are skilled in reasoning them away, hence justifying their mistreatment of their people.

So, what are the tell-tale signs that you are being treated like an option by your leaders, (your government)?

1. You're the one asking that your opinion be sought or included in the planning of things in your community or around the country. But, your leaders that make up the government of the day:

    Don't ask for your opinion and they don't care that you have one. You are pretty much non-existent when it comes to plans or events or things being done. You do all the asking and whether you have given your opinion or not, the government does whatever it wants.

2. Your call for help and plea for better quality life go unanswered. A good example here is the Marsabit residents who offered their leaders dirty water. They had asked and asked for help to access clean water but got no response from their leaders.

    Remember in the beginning when your leaders came to you asking for your vote, and you received their attention right away? Now you'll be lucky to see their faces. It'll take the next general election for you to see them again. Your calls for help and plea for things to change no longer have the same importance they used to have when they were soliciting for your vote. They aren't keen to hear from you anymore.

3. The excuses start flying – why they can't come to visit your village or your town. They just don't want to hear what you have to say, and they don't want your company right now. They are waiting until it's close to the next election. Then, they will show up with groups of *boda-boda* riders who form part of their campaign trail. Their campaign is meant to convince you to vote them back to office.

    Can you see just how stupid they think you are?

4. Interest is lacking. They no longer seem to care or want to participate in your community events. They clearly display their lack of interest. Nothing seems to make them want to help resolve the ills in your community. They don't even hide it anymore and couldn't care any less about your feelings towards that.

> *If you engage upcoming leaders who are aspiring for leadership, the old guard shows up rudely in an attempt to show that they are still in charge. Even when you have not seen them for months or heard them address the needs of your community, they still act as if you owe them allegiance.*

5. They don't engage your community or your local leaders anymore to discuss issues like safety, or help formulate regulations that require *boda-boda* riders to act like human. They don't propose severe penalties for *boda-boda* gangs that terrorize members of the public.

    If you engage upcoming leaders who are aspiring for leadership, the old guard shows up rudely in an attempt to show that they are still in charge. Even when you have not seen them for months or heard them address the needs of your community, they still act as if you owe them allegiance.

6. You are expected to fix your community problems alone. They have left everything to you. If you want to get anything done in order to achieve positive changes, maybe it's best to just remove them from the equation.

7. They are liars. Even about little silly things that generally don't make much difference, they just don't want you to know. With the lying comes secrecy. You ask questions but don't get true answers. It's all lies and cover up.

8. You are starting to feel neglected, under-appreciated by these leaders and you are unhappy about the whole experience.

   When these feelings start coming up, something has to change, or something has changed. They are an indicator that things are not good. You should always feel connected to your leaders. If you don't, perhaps it's time to discuss so as to see if something can be fixed, or it could be time to vote them out or protest the lack of fair treatment to you and to the members of your community.

9. They only come around when they want something from you (your vote). They don't come to see how things are in your community or to spend time with members of your community. They know that when they come around with empty promises, you will jump high and do whatever it is they want. Taking advantage of you is child-play to them. They have already done that so many times.

10. Control is beginning to rear its ugly head. They are taking control of you and your mind. No wonder they are able to manipulate you. And they don't care how you feel about how they treat you or what you want them to do. It's not about you and your interests anymore. It's not even about trying to improve the quality of your life or changing the horrible conditions in the community you live in. They don't really care about that much either. They do what they want.

If you recognize these signs in your leaders, either discuss them with the leaders or vote them out. You should never be treated like an option. Everyone deserves to be loved, appreciated and happy.

Remember, again, we seek happiness from inside, but you shouldn't have to dig deeper because your leaders have made you miserable or mistreated you.

In all of our relationships with our leaders, respect should be first and foremost. Demand changes that you want to see in your government. When is the best time to demand change in your country? The best time to do that is now. Why is now the best time to do it? Because you are a member of a small group of people who have become sick and tired of being sick and tired of the on-going depreciation of your country. This is the time to assume some level of responsibility and involvement in your country in order to bring about the needed change.

If you are already involved, what you need to do now is to increase your involvement. Also, make it very intentional and specific so as to hit your set targets.

CHAPTER 10

WARNING TO ALL DRIVERS IN KENYA

"Think with your head, not with your heart when dealing with boda-boda riders." – Joe K. Mungai

There is something that I believe Edward would have wanted you to know if he had an opportunity to share it with you. But since he is not here and he will never get that opportunity, I have taken it upon myself to pass that message to you.

If my brother was still alive, I would not have known what I now know. For that reason, I regard my brother's death as a sacrifice for many, therefore I wouldn't want to keep to myself the precious lessons learned. These lessons have been dearly paid for. Edward paid for them with his life. It would be selfish of me to not share them with you.

If Edward was alive, he would want your life to be spared. He would want you to know that *boda-boda* gangs are evil. As a matter of fact, who you are, whatever you do and whatever you have angers them. In their weird reasoning, they think that you are the reason they don't have the good things of life they desire. They see you as an obstacle to their success. Anything that they might sense as going good for you irks them. They loath your success. Majority of the men who killed my brother knew him. They used to see him every day on the road. I wouldn't be surprised to learn that they killed him out of jealousy, because he owned a truck and had a brother in America.

These thugs don't care to know whether what you have is yours or not. For them, the bottom line is that you shouldn't have something that they don't have themselves. If you have it, and they don't, they regard you as their enemy.

This is how twisted and distorted the minds of many members of our society are. This mentality is promoted by the wanton corruption we see all around. When you have everyone at the top (government leaders) stealing, those at the bottom who have nothing see everyone else who has something as their enemy.

The other warning comes from me. And the warning, basically is that your safety is not guaranteed by your government. When it comes to your safety as a driver in Kenya you are on your own.

This is important to know, so that you are aware that every time you are out driving, you are taking a risk on your life. Not unless you chose to ask your member of parliament to table a motion in parliament to wake the government up from its slumber. Your government has been asleep for a long time. It has done nothing to protect you from possible assaults by *boda-boda* gangs.

These gangs camouflage as transport business entities. And they hurt, maim and kill at the slightest provocation, sometimes without provocation at all. They are killers who are running amok, unrestrained. They are always on the look-out for an opportunity to hurt, maim and kill. I don't know whether they know it, but what they are doing is exactly what the devil does.

What are the works of the devil?

Jesus gave a clear and concise answer about this question in John 8.44. Confronting the hypocritical leaders of his days, Jesus told them: *"You belong to your father, the devil, and you want to carry out your father's desires. He was a murderer from the beginning, not holding to the truth, for there is no truth in him. When he lies, he speaks his native language, for he is a liar and the father of lies."*

According to Jesus, some of the works of the devil are murder and lying. These two sins summarize the character of the devil and his goals. He works to get people destroyed (that's murder), and he desires to deceive and recruit people into helping him to cause destruction (through lying). His accomplices are cruel, brutal and their way of thinking is very dark.

These two characteristics of the devil are evident in the actions of the *boda-boda* gangs. If you listen to accounts of how they operate and how they kill innocent citizens, the gravity of their devious actions will hit you hard. And how do they orchestrate their plans? They use lies. They conjure a story and get people to believe it because they (public) don't have details of the story's background. That way, they keep the public from helping those they target to maim or kill.

Two questions come to mind. First question; if Edward knew that his friends were going to leave him without making any effort to try to save his life, would he have gone out of his way to try to protect them from the blood-thirsty gang, before trying to get to Garissa Road?

Second question; if Edward knew that the gang was out not just to physically injure him but also to kill him, wound he have made that turn to reach the police from a back road, or would he have plowed through the *boda-boda* riders who were blocking his way?

My brother had a window of opportunity to escape, but he chose not to. If he had plowed through the riders who were blocking his way, it is likely that he would be alive today. But he chose to spare the lives of those who were baying for his blood. Did it cross his mind that they would violently murder him? For God, sake they knew him! That must be the reason he didn't run over the group that had blocked the road. What a shame, that his killers never paused to think why he didn't plow through them. Maybe their minds can't process noble actions. Or they were so obsessed with murder, they couldn't bring themselves to think.

If you are a driver, you have information that my brother did not have before he was murdered. If he was here, this is what he would tell you:

Think with your head, not with your heart when dealing with *boda-boda* riders.

If *boda-boda* riders make a dash at you because of a misunderstanding, thinking with your head instead of your heart might save your life. Don't expect them to reason as humans, because they won't.

Why is this warning important? I'd want someone to benefit

from the painful lessons we have learnt following the death of my brother. The difficulties, the agony and the injustice that my family has suffered might have some meaning if a life can be spared.

There is something you need to understand about this homegrown gang. *Boda-boda* gangs comprise of fierce and barbarous men who slash and kill without a second thought. I know it, because they did it to my brother. As long as you use their services, or you use Kenyans road, you need to know the dangers this homegrown terrorist group poses to you.

As shared earlier, these people are beyond any human decency that you know of. They lack ability to behave and live like human beings. They lack ability to empathize or to see things from anyone else's perceptive other than their own.

If a misunderstanding with a *boda-boda* rider ensues while on the road, don't get out of your vehicle to resolve it. *Boda-boda* riders don't reason as you do, so, don't expect them to reason as normal human beings.

It is important for you to understand that you don't have anything to do with them. You are not their savior. You cannot change them. Whilst they can modify their behavior if they so choose to, they will most likely not be influenced by your reasoning.

> *You can imagine how painful it is for me, that am using my brother's misfortune as an example to help you and probably save your life. But this is the only way I can find some meaning out of his death.*

You can imagine how painful it is for me, that am using my brother's misfortune as an example to help you and probably save your life. But this is the only way I can find some meaning out of his death.

They took pleasure in slashing, stoning, clobbering and puncturing my brother. One of them reported that they were frustrated by the fact that he was stronger than they had assumed. As a result, it took a long time to injure him enough to stop him from defending himself so he could just stay still to be killed.

They were upset by his attempts to remain alive by fighting back!

One of the people who were apprehended by members of the public detailed the way the gang killed my brother and the tools they used. He even revealed the name of the person who had the machete that was used to slash my brother.

Ask yourself; why would *boda-boda* riders need these types of weapons? Of what use are those weapons in *boda-boda* business?

The murderers had a field day as they slashed and clobbered my brother with their crude weapons. They had dragged him some distance away from his truck, to an isolated spot where help would not be easy to find. There, they inflicted maximum pain on him. Then they left him for dead.

It is torturous to imagine the pain and agony Edward suffered as he lay on the ground, bleeding profusely. He became an offering, so to say, for all the evil that has afflicted the whole nation because of lack of leadership at the local as well as national level. The murderous gang members poured all their anger, frustration and bitterness on an innocent citizen. My brother had done nothing to contribute to their anger. It is their government, which happens to be your government, that has failed to foster conditions that promote the well-being of its citizens.

It's scary to drive on Kenyan roads, knowing that these lawless gangs are freely operating on the same roads.

CHAPTER 11

THE MENACE OF BODA-BODA GOONS

"For unto whomsoever much is given, of him shall be much required."
- Luke 12:48

Knowing the way my brother was killed by a *boda-boda* gang, and having been frustrated for more than three years now by law enforcement agencies that seem more eager to protect the murderers than ensure justice is done, I regard it as my responsibility to warn all Kenyans everywhere about the dangers posed by these gangs that masquerade as business entities. If you live in Kenya, you need to be constantly conscious of the danger that lurks around, in the form of *boda-boda* riders. If you live outside Kenya, you need to be prepared to face the dangers posed by these gangs, whenever you visit Kenya. These *boda-boda* gangs operate outside the regulations that govern civilized society.

Kenyans don't enjoy their freedom or their constitutional rights anymore, because of lawless gangs. Sadly, citizens know that they can't find any reprieve in agencies that have been tasked by the constitution to protect them. My brother tried to drive to a police station when he realized that the *boda-boda* riders were out to use crude force, not reason, to resolve a minor issue. Now that he never reached the police station, the least that his family would expect the police to do is to expedite the process of justice so as to help the family sense some measure of closure. Why the police would choose to work hand-in-glove with blood-thirsty criminals is something I can't bring myself to comprehend. I know that it has everything to do with money-exchange. Has life in Kenya become so cheap?

How can a bunch of goons determine who should die and who

should live? They murder their fellow Kenyans, a crime that is punishable by law, but they do it without any fear of repercussions, because they know there will be none. And so, they kill without fear of punishment or pain. To them, murder is like sport. They do it with impunity.

Imagine the horror my brother experienced when it dawned on him that the goons would execute their evil scheme, and that there was nothing he could do to stop them, because even law enforcement agencies, with all the power vested in them, cannot stop them. Why? Because the law enforcement agencies have allied themselves with the gangsters, rather than with the public they are mandated to protect. They have surrendered their authority to the criminals. Kenyans have been put on the auction block by their leaders and those mandated to protect them. Their lives can be taken away any time, and nothing will come out of it.

I have caught a glimpse of my reflection so many times as tears stream down my face each time I imagine my brother's pain when he was faced with this reality. The knowledge and memory of this reality will be etched in my memory as long as I live. It's not something I can just decide to erase. It pains me to know that Breanna, my eight year old daughter will never see her uncle again. She met him only once. She won't have opportunity to ever meet him again, all because of the evil actions of a barbaric gang.

Let share with you briefly what hurt me most as I grieve my brother.

The Loss that Could Have Been Avoided

In my journey of grieving my brother and dealing with his loss, there is one thing that hurts me the most; the manner in which he was killed, and the apparent impunity exercised by those who did it, and also by those protecting them.

There is nothing that torments me more than knowing that the murderers inflicted so much pain on my brother while he was still alive. They cut his fingers with a machete, to stop him from fighting back as they slashed his face and crushed his jaw. They also broke off most of his teeth. Then they crushed his skull. They were eager to ensure that he would not survive, but would die a slow, painful death.

In summary, the pain that eats me up every day is the knowledge that:

- Edward was murdered in cold blood.
- His killers inflicted so much pain on him before they killed him.
- He suffered so much before he died.
- His killers knew him.
- His companions never called for help.
- He was killed for nothing.
- His killers have not faced justice.
- His killers are out and waiting to hurt another person
- The police let his killers go free.
- His local government is doing nothing about his murder.
- His chief is doing nothing about his murder.
- His community is doing nothing about his murder.
- His representative in the County Assembly is doing nothing about his murder.
- His representative in the National Assembly is doing nothing about his murder.
- Religious leaders in this region are doing nothing about his murder.
- His national government is doing nothing about his murder.
- His president is doing nothing about his murder.

Edward was a driver, and his record on the road was good. He was a good driver. And although he died while on the road, he died because criminals who don't value life murdered him. His life was cut short by *boda-boda* riders who work between Kiganjo Village and BAT bus stop at Makongeni, in Thika.

Edward's murder by *boda-boda* goons is not an isolated case. A little while after my brother's death, I received several messages from people who had their own stories to share about the agony they have suffered as a result of lawless acts by the goons. This is proof enough that the pain my family is experiencing is not peculiar to us. Many other families are experiencing similar pain. Kenyans will continue to be at the mercy of this gang until a solution is found. Below is a sample portion of one of those many messages.

Senseless Killing by *boda-boda* Riders in Kenya

Hi, Joe. This has happened again. It still haunts me because you were a victim of this boda-boda group, just the other day. I hope it's alright that I write to you about this very difficult situation. I have read what you shared with the public after you lost your brother, and am convinced that we have to continue voicing their horrible acts until something happens. That's why I am sharing this with you.

I have insisted that boda-boda riders should be treated like an organized criminal gang. They will continue killing Kenyans as long as we allow them to be a law unto themselves.

> *There is nothing that torments me more than knowing that the murderers inflicted so much pain on my brother while he was still alive. They cut his fingers with a machete, to stop him from fighting back as they slashed his face and crushed his jaw. They also broke off most of his teeth. Then they crushed his skull. They were eager to ensure that he would not survive, but would die a slow, painful death.*

Another young life has been lost because boda-boda riders decided to gang up and kill him for no reason.

Whenever one is confronted by boda-boda riders, it's always because of something that they have exaggerated to help them steal from the public or cover their evil deeds. This is thuggery at its best.

On that doomed evening, this young man, who hails from Chinga Ward, boarded a boda-boda at Murang'a where he was working as a Sales Manager with Murang'a Distributors, and was heading to his residence at Mukuyu Market, not far from Murang'a town centre.

On arrival at the estate, he allegedly gave the boda-boda guy a one thousand shillings note. When he asked for change, the boda guy said he had given him a hundred bob, so there was no change for him. An argument ensued as the young man insisted that he be given back his change. The boda-boda guy phoned his colleagues and in no time they arrived. Within no time, the story changed. The boda-boda guy started claiming that the passenger wanted to rob him of his motorcycle.

Things escalated so fast and instead of taking the passenger to the nearby police station, they beat him and set him on fire, killing him on the spot.

Surely, how do you kill a fellow human being over one thousand shillings, or two, or even ten?

And just like that, the 28 years old dad to one young boy was no more. We buried him today, so badly burnt that we had to bury him immediately the casket arrived home this morning then did the service afterwards.

It's hard to even describe the pain but our hope and prayer is that Justice will be served for this senseless killing.

My question is, where are our leaders? Where are our custodians of the law? Where is our safety and security? Who will ever change this situation?

The leaders of the communities where these evils are being perpetrated should come together and work in unison to bring this to a stop. But am afraid this has not happened. And there is no sign in the horizon that something like this is about to work or will ever happen.

As a nation, we must start devising ways of making such senseless killings come to an end. This is so traumatic and costly for families. Anyone involved in such a murder should never be allowed to engage in this business ever again. These kind of criminals should be behind bars for a long, long time, or even be sentenced to capital punishment. If we implement this strictly, people will think twice before they act so irresponsibly. We hope the investigating officers will ensure the perpetrators of this crime are brought to book, even as we pray to God to grant the affected family fortitude to bear the loss.

What do you do after reading something like that? What do you say? What would you do or say if your loved one is the victim of such acts? Put yourself in the shoes of the families that have to experience such unbearable pain. Worse than that, imagine yourself being attacked and killed in this manner. Because this can be you or me today, and others will be reading about it tomorrow.

A member of the community in Kiganjo sent me the following message, after receiving word that I was in the process of publishing a book detailing my brother's gruesome murder:

Hello, Joe. Hope you're well.

I remember that very well (my brother's murder). It was painful, heartless and barbaric. The shock was all over the neighborhood.

You've borne that pain, glad that God heals.

This is a great move to share with others and admonish too.

Looking forward to the copy.

The big lesson for all of us, is that when a society loses its morals and ethical values in pursuit of quick economic gains, and when the leadership stops applying the law and instead leaves ordinary people to their own fate, the law of the jungle fills the vacuum.

The solution is to introduce good governance and effective leadership. This is so important, because "no nation or entity can rise above the mental capacity of its decision makers."

PART 4

HOW CAN WE REDEEM OURSELVES?

In this section, I discuss two subjects that are important in guiding us towards redeeming ourselves from where we find ourselves now as a society but with a new resolute to creating a future that is of our own making. These two subjects are **Building Trust** and **The Way Forward.**

Why is this important? This is why; it goes without saying, that our country is hurting and hurting bad at many different levels. That is why we all need to come together and take action to secure a different future. Again, it goes without saying: a new future demands a new way of thinking and a new way of doing things. If we are all in this together and we want a different future, we all together have to take action. There is no shortcut to having and owning a different future. We have to act differently in order to get it.

My role here is to help raise awareness, educate and empower you with an aim to save someone's life and help millions of Kenyans find justice that they are entitled to. My brother is gone. He won't come back to us, but if the message from his death can rescue a life, then I have done my job of keeping his memory alive.

Let's unpack these two subjects together.

CHAPTER 12

BUILDING TRUST

"Injustice anywhere is a threat to justice everywhere."
– Dr. Martin Luther King Jr.

Does it upset you, when there is a genuine problem, to see government officials attaching a solution to a problem that has nothing to do with the actual problem?

That is what we have been doing in Kenya. That is what our leaders have been doing. And they have been doing this for a very long time.

How can we trust our government anymore?

Trust is something that our government owes Kenyans. Kenyans are not obligated to trust it. There is no compelling reason for them to do so. The hurt, the loss of lives and the devastation that the government has allowed to happen to them is sickening.

The government has its work cut out. It has to work very hard to build trust with its people at home and abroad, and with the whole world at large.

Kenyans deserve a government they can trust. They deserve leaders who are worth the titles they hold.

There has been a continuous erosion of public trust in politics and politicians in our country. This is a fact that the government, present and future, must address before it can convince people that it has what it takes to bring about genuine changes in the country.

I personally struggled way before my brother died to build trust with the government of Kenya. I discerned a while back that the government does not represent the will of the entire nation. It only serves the interests of a few. That is unacceptable.

The knowledge that law enforcement officers were bribed to let my brother's killers go free pains me deeply. The government continues to abuse those it has already exposed to murderous gangs.

We, the people, choose leaders who go on to form government. For so long we have listened to empty promises by our leaders. Time has come for our leaders to listen to us. We have found our voice, and intend to use it.
As a government, you have mistreated us long enough.
Look at the mountain of evidence that stands against you.
Enough is enough, we have had it with you.
We cannot take it anymore.
We have joined hands and are calling on you to act.
We are now a force and won't stop until the tables are turned.

You have no idea how it feels to be mistreated, because you thrive on the misfortunes of those who suffer injustice. As citizens, we are the people you have so heartlessly mistreated. Not only that, you have allowed other evil groups, like *boda-boda* gangs, to trample on our rights. You have left us exposed to dangers you are supposed to protect us from.

> *We, the people, choose leaders who go on to form government. For so long we have listened to empty promises by our leaders. Time has come for our leaders to listen to us. We have found our voice, and intend to use it.*

It's really hard to put in words what this feels. I cannot adequately express the level of disgust I feel when I think about the many ways our government has failed its people. I am not sure I will ever come to terms with the horrible ways our leaders have manipulated and violated us. When they come to us asking for votes, they promise to change things around, but do nothing once they assume office. Through bad governance, they continue to destroy the lives of the people they are mandated to protect.

The effects of bad governance are far-reaching. The ill-effects extend beyond the generation they negatively impact. Those who survive injustice get haunted by the experiences the rest of their lives, making it difficult for them to live quality lives. Their livelihoods nose-dive.

I don't know about you, so let me speak for myself. I am now facing my government as a survivor, not as a victim. I have regained my strength, much as I still grieve the loss of my brother.

I know that I am not alone in what I have experienced. I think suffering and anguish have become mandatory for all Kenyans. The pain is compounded by the fact that incompetence and unprofessional leadership continues unchecked through all the levels of government. This has caused Kenyans a great deal of physical, mental and emotional pain.

The government is not representing the people who elected it, neither is it fulfilling its duty. It's not addressing our concerns. Instead, it's taking advantage of us, because it knows that we think that we have no power to get ourselves out of the pit we find ourselves in.

We know that our government is wrong, but we feel guilty to think that way because we are the ones who elected the leaders who are abusing the mandate we bestowed on them. As citizens, we are hesitant to allow ourselves to believe that the problem lies with our government, which really is the case.

Imagine feeling like you have no power and no voice.

Well, as citizens we have power and we have a voice. We want our government to know that. We have both power and voice. And we are beginning to come together. Soon, our power will be felt, and our voice will be heard.

A Word of Advice to Our Government

I think that a word of advice to our government is in order. Continuing to issue empty statements and empty promises, thinking that this will pacify us as Kenyans, won't work any longer. Talk by the government has proved to be worthless. The issues we are dealing with concern lives of citizens and the future of our country. The time to act is now. This homegrown terrorist group must be stopped and silenced forever.

Only real change will boost people's trust in their government. The government must be willing to fight for its citizens.

To know what changes are needed requires us to understand what exactly happened, why it happened, and how it happened. This will be a long and painful process, but it's the only way to identify all the factors that contributed to this problem, and also educate ourselves on how to avoid it in the future.

How did the police become so corrupt, to the extent of allowing murderers to rule communities?

Who gave the police power to release murderers without taking them through court process?

What is the work of MCAs, if they cannot protect the people in the communities where they are leaders?

What is the role of members of parliament, in a situation like this?

To believe in the future of Kenyans is to believe in change, but how can we believe in change when our government is not even acknowledging the problem? It's easy to claim that citizens' safety is government's highest priority, but government has been saying that for years. It has not stopped criminal gangs from brutalizing the public.

Boda-boda Riders

Boda-boda riders should know that whatever they do cannot stop us from moving on with our lives. They have not taken our love for our country away from us. We love Kenya, and that love is stronger than the evil that resides in the criminals, and in those who enable them to hurt Kenyans.

As citizens of Kenya, we will do everything we can to ensure that these criminals don't hurt one more Kenyan. We won't rest until the criminal gangs get dismantled. We won't rest easy and watch them take away our future and that of our children. We won't allow their evil influence to impact the future generations.

They started terrorizing Kenyans several years ago. This book is probably the first documented reporting of the criminal actions of *boda-boda* gangs. If one person, just one person had summoned courage to speak and fearlessly condemn these gangs and their evil actions, maybe the tragedy that befell my brother could have been averted. And not just my brother, because I know that many innocent Kenyans have had their lives cut short by these gangs. If someone had boldly spoken out earlier, many families would have been spared the anguish they are experiencing today.

As citizens of Kenya, we will do everything we can to ensure that these criminals don't hurt one more Kenyan. We won't rest until the criminal gangs get dismantled. We won't rest easy and watch them take away our future and that of our children. We won't allow their evil influence to impact the future generations.

I wish one *boda-boda* rider would come forward and answer this one question; how do you sleep at night after maiming or killing an innocent citizen? You have been allowed to use the same roads that other right-thinking citizens use. You live amongst innocent citizens who don't know the philosophy that runs your lives. You are trusted by so many Kenyans who come to you as passengers in need of transport, convinced that it's better to use your service instead of walking, especially at night. They come to you hoping to be protected from the same heinous crimes you end up subjecting them to.

I cringe, knowing the danger that many innocent Kenyans – those who use your services and those who use the same roads you use – are exposed to. You are supposed to help the public have easier means of transport. This is a privilege that you have abused, and continue to abuse.

We want you to know that your days, and the days of those in corridors of power who help you conceal your evil deeds, are numbered. Your day of reckoning is here. This time, you won't escape the brutal force of justice.

CHAPTER 13

THE WAY FORWARD

"I can't take back the past, but I can fight for the future."
– Shannon A. Thompson

As Kenyans, we have been fooled for pretty long. We have been fooled to believe empty promises given by our leaders. What has happened to us because of believing those empty promises?

This is what has happened: without knowing, we have been forced into a relationship with imposters and corrupt leaders. And so, now, we have become their accomplices. As George Orwell remind us, "A people that elect corrupt politicians, imposters, thieves and traitors are not victims but accomplices."

What have we gained from this relationship?

This relationship has caused us to suffer incredibly. We are paying dearly for failing to make a break with bad leaders. It has cost many Kenyans their lives. The future of our children is in jeopardy. Our leaders have used this relationship to manipulate us. That's why this relationship must end. We must find a way out of this mess.

A number of people in Kenya and some in the diaspora have given up, there are a few left who believe that it's still possible for us to redeem ourselves from this mess.

I am one of the few who believe that we can redeem ourselves. We cannot throw in the towel and we cannot concede defeat. This is our fight. It's true that we are up against heavy odds, but giving up won't remove the evil from our midst. Giving up will empower and embolden those seeking to destroy our communities.

As a people and as a country, we need to get ourselves out of the muck and mire we have gotten ourselves into. I believe that together, we can truly change Kenya. Now, more than ever before, we need to stand up and speak up, in order to pull our country back from the edge. The time to act is now.

Allow me to ask you one question, my fellow Kenyans; why are you so afraid of freedom? Why is the idea of being free so appalling? This is what everyone wants in every other corner of the world. Everyone wants to be free. And part of being free involves asking our leaders why something is not the way it ought to be. It involves demanding an explanation.

What is our problem?

Our problem is indifference. We are indifferent in the face of poverty, starvation and cruelty – all caused by our leaders. We are indifferent to the fact that our jails are full of petty thieves while the grand thieves have a field day, enjoying their freedom.

That is our problem.

Sorry to be the bearer of bad news. But living our lives like this is costing us too much and costing our children their future. We all must realize that nothing great has ever been achieved except by those who dare believe that something inside them is more superior than their prevailing circumstances. Our leaders have caged us in. They want us to remain quiet and toe the line without challenging the kind of life they have subjected us to.

> *We need to trust each other once again. We need to regain trust in humanity. We need to believe that someone will respond when needed to respond. We need to believe that people will regard the lives of others as much as their own.*

It is time we let our leaders know that we have had enough of that, we won't take it any longer.

The Political Swamp

As my friend Pastor Brad Sherman would say, corrupt political systems are often referred to as swamps. And it's not difficult to see why; there are so many parallels. When someone dares to cut a ditch through the political swamp as you would do on a physical swamp to drain it, the swamp creatures who live there, especially the creatures deep below, get nervous and start to panic. Fearing that they are about to be exposed, they resort to irrational behavior, much like fish trapped in puddles of shallow water after a ditch has been cut through a swamp, frantically flipping their "tales," notwithstanding the fact that their lies become more and more obvious. It's all they know to do. That's why all we hear from them are empty promises.

These leaders will lift up a finger to do the work they get paid only when a Kenyan has coughed some money to bribe and oil their hands.

This is absurdity.

Pastor Brad draws from lessons learned while growing up in an area that was largely a swamp-land in Southeast Missouri. Swamp draining, he says, is nasty work, but it's necessary work. How does this analogy illuminate the political conditions of Kenya and the amount of work that is needed to be done? Majority of Kenyans don't know just how nasty things are, that's why it's important to expose the filth and stench of a corrupt and evil machinery.

Pastor Brad further says: "In the farming industry, draining a swamp is worth the effort, because swamp land is fertile soil with great production potential." Likewise, the swampy landscape of the government has great potential for good, but it requires good people who will sow good seed, and be good stewards of the land.

We need to raise awareness about the horrific and vile things that are happening across the whole country. To this end, we need persistent and courageous swamp drainers who will stay the course. We all have a part to play in cleaning this mess. While at it, we need to remember the swamp drainers; they need our support. Be light. Walk in truth. Pray that evil will be exposed. Get involved by bringing godly principles to government at local and national levels. Do not give up on Kenya. This nation will enter her destiny and become a productive land, a blessing to the nations.

Be part of the few that are busy working with God to destroy the works of the devil. Scripture says: *"The reason the Son of God appeared was to destroy the works of the devil."* (1 John 3:8b).

A swamp is usually a dark place, Pastor Brad asserts, and draining it is largely about exposing it to the light. This is how we become workers together with God, by exposing the nasty work of darkness. We won't know just how much nasty it is until we begin to stir the muck at the bottom. That's when we'll discover the real filth and stench of the swamp (deep state), and those it protects. If you think they are nasty now, just wait! Things will probably look worse before they look better, as the end of the swamp draws near. But do not be deterred by their antics. Ignore their lies and intimidation, their empty promises and bold posturing. Once exposed, it is easy to deal with them. In the end, predators become prey as they turn against each other.

We are called to expose the works of darkness. *"Walk as children of light (for the fruit of the Spirit is in all goodness, right-eousness, and truth), finding out what is acceptable to the Lord. And have no fellowship with the unfruitful works of darkness, but rather expose them,"* (Ephesians 5:8-11).

Be Your Brothers' Keeper

We need to trust each other once again. We need to regain trust in humanity. We need to believe that someone will respond when needed to respond. We need to believe that people will regard the lives of others as much as their own.

We need to walk and drive on our roads in Kenya without asking ourselves every minute we are there, "Are the *boda-boda* men on this road part of the gang or not?"

We need to feel and be safe again. This is not something we should be bargaining for. This is our right as citizens of Kenya.

New and Improved Services

The government needs to establish new and improved services that are meaningful to its people. If not, they all should resign and let the citizens elect new, responsible and accountable leadership.

In the introduction to this chapter, I reminded you how we have been fooled by our leaders, and how these leaders have taken advantage of us. This, as I mentioned, has caused us to suffer incredible losses.

The losses we have suffered cannot be undone. Beating ourselves up for allowing ourselves to be manipulated won't help. But we can change our future by demanding new and better conditions in our country. We can demand that all corrupt leaders be fired. We can force them out now. Or refuse to elect them again in future.

I have to remind my fellow Kenyans and even broadly all Africans with whom I share a common bond, that ignoring corrupt government officials and evil gangs doesn't make them go away. This approach has been tried before. The outcome has been catastrophic.

We have to make it very clear to our leaders, that we won't put up with their conduct anymore. We are not going to elect them or their kind anymore. Why? They have continually used the power we hand them to inflict pain on us and destroy our future. We'll cut loose and ensure they no longer manipulate or control us. This will give us freedom and space to think about our needs and the future of our children.

Now, let's go do it. You and I are members of a community of change-makers.

If there was ever a time to take part in the transformation that our country longs for, this is it! If you have a passion to serve your country and create a better future for your children and future generations, opportunities await you.

If we each take our position and do our part in this new change that we are demanding, together, we can achieve something positive. Something better. Something worthwhile for the next generation. And remember, the next generation is made up of our own children. We must not fail them. Let's stand our ground, and fight for them.

A SPECIAL INVITATION

SPEAK OUT FOR A LIFE INTERNATIONAL (SOLI)

"Without a sense of caring, there can be no sense of community."
– Anthony. D. Angelo

SOLI

Vision: To change the lives of people and improve their communities.

Mission: Provide advocacy & education against harassment, oppression and violence, wherever they occur, whether at home, at work or on the streets.

Allow me to introduce you to SOLI, a nonprofit that is geared to helping people around the world in improving the conditions of their lives and their communities.

SOLI is a non-partisan, issues-based organization. We work to educate communities and candidates alike across the political spectrum in order to change the systems and narratives that oppress communities. We believe that together we can organize to make real, lasting change.

The first aspect of our work is to wake people up from their dream-like trance that prevents them from seeing their true value and their life's purpose on the face of the earth.

Our goal is to educate people to know their rights. It's our desire that you attain this knowledge because this is going to empower you. When you know your rights. You can better protect yourself, your family and your community.

Speak Out, Speak Up for a Life
Even if it's not for yourself (and you should speak out on your behalf too), learn how to speak out on behalf of another person. It's important and healthy to do so.

SOLI is out on a mission to change the lives of people around the world, one life at a time.

The broken government systems and the deteriorating conditions of life that you see around you will never improve unless someone speak out about them. It is our responsibility to shine the light on them so as to raise awareness among a wide circle of citizens. That way, we'll demand accountability and get our leaders involved. Engaging with candidates is an important aspect of holding elected officials accountable once they get elected.

Why is knowledge of issues of concern important? It's because, knowledge is not only power but also eye-opening. Once knowledge provides you with facts, you are able to see the big picture. When you see these issues, speak out about them. Or about what you hope to see happen. Or about what you believe is possible. You will discover that authentic and unbiased sharing of issues with others can inspire new perspectives to your hearers.

A lot of people have no clue about the issues of concern that you see every day. That's why you need to share with them about what's happening. Don't rob them of that opportunity by failing to share what you observe every day. Together, let's grab hold of our voices of change, and truly change Kenya.

There are no two ways about it; we have to work together to bring about the change we want to see. Empty promises by our leaders will not cut it, neither will they be acceptable anymore. We have to demand concrete action from our leaders and government.

Join and support SOLI and help make this change possible. Let's change our lives and the lives of our families and those of our neighbors. Let's engage in action that can change our fate and the fate of so many other people. SOLI is your partner if you have a deep-seated belief that every Kenyan should have access to a better life, a life that is free from harassment, discrimination, oppression and violence. My uncle reminded me not long ago that, the strongest people make time to help others even when they are struggling with their own problems.

We have created an online community of like-minded individuals to help you start your own positive ripples. The community (speak out speak up for a life community) was designed with you in mind. You will experience the power of association by being part of a positive community where you will be able to interact with others and touch their lives, and also share your own stories. You can be a part of a movement – a movement that can make a difference in our individual nations and in the world as a whole. The reason I encourage you to join this movement is because of the ripple effect we can create together. The ripple effect that comes from our combined effort is so much bigger than the individual ripples we create. Our effectiveness lies in the collective ripples we will create together in our nation.

It is my deepest desire that you leave a legacy of positive ripples.

Become a change agent and help SOLI transform lives.

To join the like-minded individuals community, visit: speakout-speakup.life or contact us on contact@speakoutspeakup.life

You can also follow us on Facebook - **www.facebook.com/yourspeakout** and Twitter - **www.twitter.com/yourspeakout**

I look forward to seeing you there!

www.ingramcontent.com/pod-product-compliance
Lightning Source LLC
Chambersburg PA
CBHW060511280326
41933CB00014B/2917